Children of the Poor

Also by Mike Moore:

On Balance
Beyond Today
The Added Value Economy
The Pacific Parliament
Hard Labour
Fighting for New Zealand

CHILDREN OF THE POOR

How Poverty Could Destroy New Zealand's Future

MIKE MOORE

CANTERBURY UNIVERSITY PRESS

First published in 1996 by
CANTERBURY UNIVERSITY PRESS
University of Canterbury
Private Bag 4800
CHRISTCHURCH

ISBN 0-908812-67-1

Typeset and designed by Richard King
Jacket design by G. & A. Nelson
Printed by GP Print

Dedicated to the children of the poor,
and to those in business who will create the jobs
and the wealth that will offer the best hope
for the children of the poor to get their fair share
of the Kiwi Dream.

contents

introduction

WORDS MATTER. Books can create the conditions for change. Books can ignite a nation's conscience. Charles Dickens' vivid description of poverty shamed smug Victorian Britain. It made the country aware of the two nations that lived side by side in the capital of the wealthiest, most powerful empire history had ever known. Dickens' first paragraph from *A Tale of Two Cities* resonates down through the generations. It is as applicable in 1996 as it was when it was first written in 1859:

> It was the best of times, it was the worst of times, it was the age of wisdom, it was the age of foolishness, it was the epoch of belief, it was the epoch of incredulity, it was the season of Light, it was the season of Darkness, it was the spring of hope, it was the winter of despair, we had everything before us, we had nothing before us, we were all going direct to Heaven, we were all going direct the other way . . .

British social reformers expressed their outrage, church leaders sermonised from pulpits and politicians realised that two societies could not live in peace side by side. One half free, healthy and wealthy; the other an underclass – poor, uneducated, sick and exploited. An economic revolution had taken place. Britain had evolved from an agricultural society to an industrial society. The class war had arrived. The social solidarity of workers who lived in mill and mining towns was stirring and beginning to get restless and organised.

Benjamin Disraeli, later to become one of Britain's greatest prime ministers, wrote the novel *Sybil*. A clever book full of wit, charm, romance and political intrigue, it questioned the values of Victorian Britain. Clichés only become clichés because they are in the main true. Disraeli's phrase 'Two Nations' has passed into the English language. He warned Britain of the obscene inequalities of the day – from the desperate poverty of industrial workers to the absurd and flamboyant excesses of the very rich.

A passage from his novel reads:

> 'Well, society may be in its infancy,' said Egremont slightly smiling, 'but say what you like, our Queen reigns over the greatest nation that ever existed.'
>
> 'Which nation?' asked the younger stranger, 'for she reigns over two.'
>
> The stranger paused; Egremont was silent, but looked enquiringly.
>
> 'Yes,' resumed the younger stranger after a moment's interval. 'Two nations; between whom there is no intercourse and no sympathy; who are as ignorant of each other's habits, thoughts, and feelings, as if they were dwellers in different zones, or inhabitants of different planets who are formed by a different breeding, are fed by a different food, are ordered by different manners, and are not governed by the same laws.'
>
> 'You speak of. . .' said Egremont, hesitatingly.
>
> 'THE RICH AND THE POOR.'

Disraeli's vision of a Tory Britain, a property-owning democracy, won through. This probably saved Britain from the violent revolutions that later shook much of the European world.

Several generations later in New Zealand, a radical young agitator, hardened by the experiences of the trenches of the First World War and disgusted by depression and personal poverty, wrote an explosive novel. John A. Lee's *Children of the Poor* described a painful personal journey from poverty that shook New Zealand and helped propel him into Parliament and Labour into power in 1935. New Zealanders were complacent, proud that in 'God's Own Country', a green and pleasant land that was more British than Britain, they didn't have the problems of the old world. That was not so then. Alas, nor is it so now.

In the 1920s and 1930s men and women of concern and conscience asked how people could starve amidst plenty. After the Second World War, people reasoned that if nations could unite and mobilise for war, why couldn't united nations mobilise to eradicate want and fear? The state's role in the affairs of people was legitimised by the deadly and successful struggle against fascism.

New Zealanders have become smug again. We lecture the world about our economic reforms. National pride has replaced reason and reality. A free-market economy is based on confidence. Words are no longer empty: what politicians promise, and more importantly what business people and commentators say about the state of New Zealand, matters. Interest rates and the dollar will move if confidence drops. This can stifle debate, and therefore democracy. Corporate boards have become reluctant to criticise economic policy, especially the Reserve Bank's monetary policies. Like blackbirds on a powerline, they sit or fly off, frightened together.

It is considered unpatriotic to speak or write of poverty in a nation rich enough to feed most of the world. And it has become fashionable to blame the victims. Bad parents and lazy people are seen as the problem. Every great lie must have a grain of truth to make it believable. But there are no guilty babies, no guilty children.

There are special groups such as trade unions, the Business Roundtable, women's groups, gay rights groups, environmental advocates, horse-protection leagues and Maori activists, that demand action for their vested interests. That's part of the democratic process. But who speaks for the children? I hope the facts will speak for themselves. I have borrowed John Lee's title *Children of the Poor* because it is appropriate, real and makes the point that for too many, the last 70 years have not seen much progress.

Charles Dickens wrote that it was the best of times, it was the worst of times. He wrote of a tale of two cities. The 1990s in New Zealand are the best of times for some, but the worst of times for too many. We have two cities, two nations. Some live in the shining city on a hill as prophesied by idealistic political prophets. But for too many it is a mirage. Alan Duff's book *Once Were Warriors* was a Dickensian documentary. As a movie, it motivated many to go into theatres and witness a stunning world of which they knew little. Audiences quickly filed out shaken, but not stirred into action.

Lesley Max's well-researched book *Children: Endangered Species?* brought to the public's attention unbearable facts that too many just didn't want to hear. In the midst of plenty, something has gone terribly wrong in New Zealand. Her book stands alongside those of Dickens, Disraeli and John A. Lee as a wake-up call. It woke me up. I hope this modest effort wakes up even more people.

New Zealand is the most dangerous place in the world if you are young, male and suicidal. The suicide rate for our children is the highest in the Western world. Teenage pregnancy is higher among New Zealand Maori girls than African Americans. Fifty percent of New Zealand children have experienced drugs or been in a situation where drugs have been used by the age of fifteen. Nine hundred and thirty violent crimes were committed by youngsters under fourteen in one year. One in three Kiwi kids lives in poverty. One-quarter of New Zealand children live in families where the parents or parent has no paid work. Forty thousand food parcels a month are given to families. Special-needs grant applications for food and clothing have reached 900,000 over the last four years. They have doubled in the past eighteen months. Food banks are now common place, and up to a third of new clients are employed. The Public Health Commission has reported that 22,000 children go to school hungry. One in three schools provides free food to some students. Many schools now operate soup kitchens.

A quarter of school children in South Auckland have never been to a beach. This year two schools reported that 80 percent of students were 'functionally illiterate'. Last year police reported 272 cases of children under the age of fourteen being left home alone. Nine thousand children are suspended from school each year. Twenty thousand children play truant from school every day, and the ages of truants are getting younger. Among the developed industrial nations, New Zealand has the sixth-highest infant death rate from child abuse. In a twelve-month period, Social Welfare receives more than 30,000 formal complaints of abuse, neglect and behaviour problems.

Lesley Max said in her book: 'In an age when we have at last developed sensitivity towards women, ethnic minorities, the handicapped, those with different sexual orientation, and even towards animals and the natural environment, we have hardened our hearts against the deeper needs of children, especially when those needs conflict with the needs or ideologies of adults.'

I hope this book helps set a fresh agenda for New Zealand politicians and policy- makers. It was a disgrace that the most recent election was not about the children. When we can fill halls to speak about children's rights the way Grey Power has managed to do for its members, or have as big an impact on policy as the Business Roundtable, then we will have begun to solve the problem. One which, if unaddressed, will change the nature of New Zealand society.

A reckless, reactionary reversal from an open market to a closed economy will not help the children or create new wealth and jobs. It will do the opposite. Nations that embrace trade win; those that don't, lose. After the industrial revolution it took Britain 58 years to double the real income received by each worker. America took 42 years and Japan 34 years. South Korea acheived it in eleven years after opening its economy, and China took just six years.

The difference between North and South Korea is like night and day. North Korea can't feed itself, it is polluted, its human-rights record is among the worst in the world, and because of its economic failures and its nuclear industry, it is a threat to world peace. It is a closed and frightened society. Former South Korean presidents are now before the courts. The country is not perfect by Western standards, but its future is clear. South Korea now takes as much of the New Zealand export market as does England. The United Kingdom took 90 percent of our exports 50 years ago; now it takes about 10 percent.

The economic facts of history are clear. To close down a market economy because it fails the bottom 20 percent of the population would be a catastrophe, just as not doing more for those 20 percent who are losing out would be a disaster.

This book warns against a reactionary economic reversal, and explains how we can expand our economy to look after more people and provide the wealth to save the children of the poor. We *can* have our cake and eat it too.

one

The Lucky Country No Longer

FOR MANY, the Kiwi dream of a job, a home, someone to love and something to hope for has become a nightmare, a mirage that keeps moving away the closer you get to it.

The poverty and squalor of one demeans us all. It is a matter of national shame to see citizens going through rubbish bins, or proud mothers asking for food from a foodbank or a blanket from a church. When I first became a member of Parliament, local priests and pastors would bring people to see me so I could help with a home, a payment or a job. Now I take people to the local churches to see if they can help. New Zealand, along with other Western economies, has moved from an agricultural to an industrial, and now to an information-based economy. In the old industrial economy there was social solidarity. There were freezing works, timber and mill towns. People joined the union, drank at the local pub or workingmen's and footy clubs. We worked, played and prayed together. There was class solidarity. We knew what one another earned.

The paradox of the information age is that we have become strangers. Most of us could name more people in *Coronation Street* and *Shortland Street* than in our own streets. Television has reduced us to an audience of one. Often neighbours and friends do not know of the silent suffering of what Mother Theresa called the most deadly disease of all – loneliness. Frequently nowadays there is no immediate family to share the problem and the pain. Behind the drawn blinds, many people live out lonely lives in quiet desperation.

I recall the case of a middle manager who, after being made redundant, for months got dressed, each day and left home to a job that didn't exist. He didn't tell his wife or his children. His lonely shame was sad, unnecessary, but real. So many New Zealanders live their lives happy and oblivious to the growing dark side of poverty, its impact and implications. It is real, painful and destructive.

A study published earlier this year found that about one third of all New Zealand children live below the poverty line. The study was carried out by the Reverend Charles Waldegrave of the Lower Hutt Family Centre, Paul Frater of Business Economic Research Limited (Berl) and Bob Stephens of Victoria University's commerce and administration department. It found that 18.5 percent of households and 25 percent of all people were below the poverty threshold. Single-parent households with children were the largest household type living in poverty, with almost three out of four single parents living below the poverty line. The study found that 64 percent of families renting homes from Housing New Zealand were below the poverty threshold. The researchers also revealed that Maori were two and a half times as likely to live in poverty as were Pakeha families, and Pacific Island families three and a half times as likely.

A study of Wellington beneficiaries commissioned by the Anglican church revealed that most households had an average of $10 or less a day to spend on food. Sixty percent had problems affording housing, 17 percent lived in overcrowded accommodation, 14 percent had no washing machine, 33 percent no carpet, 9 percent no electric jug and 6 percent no heater. Almost six out of ten beneficiaries went without necessary clothes and shoes.

A good example of the lack of understanding of poverty among those with money was the advice given to the poor at the beginning of this winter by the acting chief executive of United Electricity in Dunedin: he suggested that poor people could have water heated from 11 pm to 7 am at a cheaper rate, then use it later to run their dishwashers and nightstore heaters. Welfare workers in the city pointed out that most of the people they deal with do not have dishwashers and use cold water for washing clothes.

One constituent told me she took the kids swimming in summer to save power. People can't afford a deposit on a night heater, let alone the money to purchase one. When the fridge or iron breaks down, people go without or buy another second-hand one, hoping it will be better than the first.

I led trade missions overseas with many hard-nosed businesspeople. My heart would burst with pride when I heard them talk of New Zealand. They would say it was a good country to bring up kids: quiet and peaceful, the police didn't have guns, there was no real poverty and race relations were good. When you ask Kiwis who have been overseas for the first time what shook them most, many will say it was the first time they saw a policeman with a gun or someone sleeping on the street within a mile of Buckingham Palace or the White House. Or it might have been the first time they saw a bag lady; or an ex-mental patient walking in circles, unmedicated, talking to himself. Once when I was in India, an exporter told me he had met a beggar who held out her baby and pleaded for money. He gave her some money. She gave him the child. He was shattered.

From the frequent traveller to the person on a first-time trip, we knew what we didn't like. Grateful to be New Zealanders, whatever our political philosophies, we knew what was right and what was wrong. Our values united us. It was the New Zealand way.

We have taken the social success of our grandparents for granted. This was a country where Jack wasn't as good as his master. He was a bloody sight better! And woe betide the politician who forgot that. The lessons of Savage, Holyoake, Nash, Marshall, Kirk and even Muldoon have been forgotten. The Lucky Country is no longer. Solidarity through shared values has gone, but the romantic myth still lingers on.

Poverty, like wealth, is not just inherited. It is created by people, so it can be changed by them too. It is also the result of accidents, sickness or even old age. The welfare state was created to do away with the ancient fears of old age, sickness or accident. Old age ought to be a time of warm memories and grandchildren; an autumn of reflection on a life's work. Instead it has become a time of fear. Fear that people won't enjoy their grandchildren because if they get sick, they may have to sell their homes after an operation.

The health system is making the winter of our elderly

citizens' lives colder and more vulnerable, even a time of fear. Constituents ask me how they will pay their rest-home fees; they are concerned that they will use all their savings for their hospital care or worry what will happen to their widow. This is theft from the grandchildren. Many of us live just one traffic accident away from poverty. Illness is tough enough, but when benefits go down and state-house rentals go up to market rates, imagine the problems. Think of the implications for a family if tragedy strikes, or a child is born disabled, or with a psychiatric problem. Should that mean instant poverty?

A headmaster told me the story of an ambitious school girl whose mum and dad were unemployed. She told her teacher that she was the only one out of bed when she went to school. Think about that. She gets up, dresses, feeds herself, arranges a school lunch and goes to school. Don't her parents have the love, the will, the purpose, the drive to help her through? If not, why not?

We are now beginning to reap the social harvest of second-generation unemployment, third-generation drug taking and even third-generation gang membership. This social decay comes from apathy, failure and surrender. The victims are sneered at and called no-hopers. Where there is no hope, the cycle continues. Neglect prospers and ambitions perish, with predictable results.

Who do we blame, if anyone? Maybe everyone! There is enough blame for all of us to share. 1996 is International Year for the Eradication of Poverty, but the government has been silent for good reason. New Zealand has developed an underclass of poor. It sits, silent, like a time-bomb ticking away, lodged next to the heart of the nation. Before it goes off, let's explode some myths about New Zealand and equality. Lesley Max summed it all up in sixteen words: 'The poorest New Zealanders of all are children. The poorest children are those of solo mothers.'

She cited Dr Zoe During, a former senior medical officer of health in South Auckland, who explained that for children, poverty means 'being dirty, smelly, with recurrent skin infections, untreated impetigo, scabies and lice, with chronically discharging ears, running noses, bronchitis and attacks of gastroenteritis. It means no toys and being often left at home unattended. Bedtime is when you fall asleep looking at television.

Meals are disorganised and inadequate. There are no toothbrushes, one grey communal towel, an unclean lavatory and perhaps toddlers' and animals' excreta around the outside or even inside. It means being in trouble at school because of aggression or being ignored because of excessive shyness.'

Figures I obtained from parliamentary questions to the social welfare minister show that from 1992/93 to 1995/96, Income Support approved a staggering 745,666 food grants and 94,955 clothing grants. Another 64,601 applications for food grants were turned down. Over a third of the three-quarters of a million food grant approvals were made in the last financial year. In 1995/96, the annual number of food grants was 289,521 – more than double the number in the 1992/93 year.

There has been much boasting about the economic recovery, but the devastating thing about these figures is that they are getting worse. For the children of beneficiaries, poverty is increasing. The number of grant requests is proof of a systematic need for extra assistance on top of low wages and benefits. Every application for a grant represents a New Zealand family that cannot make ends meet.

For many New Zealanders it is the best of times, but for many it is the worst. Affluence and squalor live side by side. It is clear that very large numbers of people are hurting and have missed out horribly on New Zealand's economic recovery. Benefits are now so low and food grants so common we must conclude that the government and the treasury are operating a *de facto* food-voucher system. National has introduced ACT policies by stealth.

It is not only the government's figures that reveal alarming levels of poverty. On top of this surge in demand for Income Support grants is an explosion in food-bank usage. Food banks have been described as the most visible face of poverty in New Zealand. They are the only banks we now own. Only a few food banks existed before National's election in 1990 on the hollow promise of a 'Decent Society'. The first food bank in Auckland appeared in 1980, although researcher Adrian Whale noted in a 1993 thesis that throughout the 1980s, food banks were 'predominantly small-scale appendages to welfare services offered by city missions and other voluntary organisations'. But in the early 1990s, food banks established 'a significant presence among the range of welfare providers in the community'. At least 70 percent of food requests to the Salvation Army in 1992 were to support families with children. Figures from Presbyterian Support Services show that the number of food banks in the Auckland metropolitan area grew from 16 in 1989 to 130 in 1994.

The explosion in the number of people forced to use food banks since 1990 is the direct result of the National government's benefit cuts. The Department of Social Welfare admitted this in a report released under the Official Information Act. The report said food banks underwent a period of accelerated growth during the early 1990s, and 'it is likely that much of it was driven by the benefit cuts of April 1991'. The benefit cuts were vicious. Single parents with one child lost $27.21 net per week from their basic income. What other group in society has so cruelly been singled out for such an assault? It is economic apartheid.

Statistics New Zealand figures show that within two years from March 1990, the number of children in households receiving the bottom fifth of income had rocketed by 31 percent. That represented more than 60,000 children in just two years. Sally Jackman's 1993 research into poverty in New Zealand showed that, despite consumer prices rising 1.7 percent between March 1991 and March 1992, the average aggregate spending fell 5.3 percent in nominal terms, and more if the effects of inflation are included. Single parents were particularly hard hit, with their household expenditure falling by 13.5 percent. The best economist and minister of finance doesn't sit in Treasury or in the Beehive. She sits alone every day at a kitchen table, balancing a tiny budget. Juggling cents and dollars. Single parents' budgets must balance: they have no choice.

Salvation Army figures are equally revealing. They show that 10,261 people received food assistance in the first quarter of 1992, compared with just 2124 in the quarter immediately preceding the benefit cuts. A Lower Hutt food bank distributed 4400 food parcels in the year to June 1994, compared with just 640 in 1989. The director of Wellington's Inner City Ministry (now the Downtown Ministry) estimated in 1993 that the nation's food banks were handing out as many as 35,000 food parcels each month.

Solo mothers are among the largest users of food banks. A

report in the *Social Policy Journal of New Zealand* in December 1995 also noted that families with larger numbers of children appeared disproportionately among the pool of foodbank users, as did Maori and Pacific Island families.

Changes to the criteria for Income Support Service food grants at the end of 1994 seemed to temporarily ease the demand on food banks, although the Christchurch City Missioner, Canon David Morrell, noted that the change merely enabled the mission's foodbank to 'level peg' with the year before. Recent reports suggest that demand is as strong as ever. The Salvation Army's community and family services centre in Christchurch handed out twice as many food parcels in April 1996 as it did in April 1995, and the city's Methodist Mission distributed food parcels to 176 families in May 1996, a 38 percent increase on the year before. Further south, people were reported to have walked long distances through snow, in freezing temperatures, to reach food banks in Dunedin. A food bank spokesperson told the *Otago Daily Times* that such journeys were not unusual: 'If they can't afford the bus fare, that's it.' *The Press* reported that a 70-year-old man who went to the Methodist Mission for a blanket in May 1996 was too proud to accept food. As Canon Morrell has pointed out, visiting a food bank can be a humiliating experience: People 'don't volunteer for it as readily as one might think'.

The poor people forced to use food banks are not the only ones feeling the pressure of poverty. Church leaders are starting to talk openly about 'compassion fatigue'. Deacon Chris Wood of Wellington's Laing's Road Methodist Church told the *Evening Post:* 'Churches largely made up of ageing, declining congregations who may be struggling themselves financially are feeling the burden of ongoing social services.' Some, like Robert Hopkirk of the Presbyterian-Methodist Public Questions Committee, are beginning to ask whether community organisations and churches should be running food banks at all. Deacon Wood urged the government to join voluntary agencies to provide life's necessities for the poor, noting that the Income Support Service was 'just across the road from us, but there is no communication'. Government agencies now direct citizens – who are now called 'clients' – to charitable agencies.

It is hardly surprising that these pleas to the National government have fallen on deaf ears. Senior government MPs such as John Carter have accused church leaders of encouraging dependency on food banks with their 'constant bleating about poverty' – as though proud parents enjoy dressing their children from church shops! So it is all the fault of the churches. But where would we be without them? Prime Minister Jim Bolger, who conveniently called church leaders together for a summit just before the 1993 election, recently denied the existence of poverty in New Zealand, and said that parents were to blame if their children went to school hungry.

Poverty is now hitting more than those on benefits and the unemployed. Food banks are reporting growing numbers of people in paid employment knocking on their doors for food. This disturbing trend was confirmed by a national survey carried out by the Labour party in early 1996, which found that up to 20 percent of people requesting handouts from Salvation Army food banks had jobs.

As Labour's employment spokesperson, Steve Maharey, pointed out, the disposable income of the poorest 20 percent of wage and salary earners is being whittled away by market rents for state houses, higher school fees and increased health charges. The Employment Contracts Act (ECA) has created an Americanised labour market where temporary and part-time workers are being employed on a casual basis on low wages. That is why food banks are now finding workers to be a sizeable portion of their clientele. As Steve said, 'The working poor is no longer a phenomenon of foreign slums; it is now hitting home.'

The ECA has achieved the opposite of what its authors promised. Those who believe in the majestic wisdom of the market and competitive forces must now acknowledge that the result of the ECA has been a steady one-sided devaluation of labour, its costs and conditions. Such an environment works for business for a short time. Labour is cheaper and profits higher. But in the long run it is not the cost of labour that determines competitiveness. If it was, Ethiopia would have the lowest unemployment in the world. Lowering labour costs, just like cutting back on training, upskilling and research and development, makes a balance sheet look better for a few years, but then what? It is ultimately bad for business because if all we have to offer the world is a cheaper pair of hands, then what? Productivity and output per person are what matters, not the lowest wage on the block. The ECA is unfair and puts too much power in the hands of employers. Most bosses are good, but when their competitors cut wages, good employers can be forced to follow suit just to stay afloat. It is not right that low-paid workers continue to make sacrifices and then see multi-million dollar handouts to top executives.

The gap between top executives' and workers' incomes has exploded. Workers no longer believe that hard work and commitment to a business will be rewarded. Rather, the employer will reward him or herself based on how many workers can be shed. The most ruthless managers who try the hardest to prove their 'managerial skills' and win fat bonuses are now to be found in the public service.

Equality of sacrifice is the key to social cohesion and an economic partnership. YWCA national director Marion Wood makes the point thus: 'While the whole of New Zealand is watching open-mouthed as businessmen involved in the Winebox inquiry fight to retain what they consider to be their legal entitlements, the Business Roundtable has the gall to attack beneficiaries who are trying to get their legal entitlements and the voluntary groups who are supporting them.' She was responding to a Roundtable report which suggested that a greater share for beneficiaries in the economic recovery would erode the cultural basis for both economic growth and social cohesion.

The much-vaunted tax-cut package of July 1996 was no help to most of the poor. It drove a wedge between the working poor and those who had no jobs, not even a low-paid job. The National government's budget was, according to people like Chris Wood, 'a missed chance to address poverty in New Zealand'. She thought it unacceptable that a nation with a $3 billion budget surplus 'looks the other way when faced with the existence of poverty'.

The Budget was cleverly mocked by food bank representatives who held two cans of baked beans outside Parliament to show what families on benefits could buy with the extra $2.50 they would receive in family support. The underlying Budget message, according to Sharon Torstonson, executive director of the Council of Social Services in Christchurch, was that 'you are worthless unless you earn a wage'. She told *The Press* that the Budget 'totally devalues the contribution made by beneficiaries and superannuitants to the country. Superannuitants built New Zealand and sole parents are raising the next generation in very trying circumstances.'

Auckland University economics lecturer Susan St John summed up the plight of the children of the poor in an article published in the *New Zealand Herald*: 'It is hard to imagine why anyone would design a payment to assist with the costs of children in low-income families that actually disappears when the family falls on hard times. Nevertheless, that is what has happened.'

She pointed out that families that did not qualify because they were described as 'dependent on the state' would miss out on an independent tax credit worth $7.50 per child per week (rising to $15 from July 1997). So, for example, a mother in a low-income family of four would find that her extra $30 a week tax credit would disappear when her husband became unemployed or was unfortunate enough to be disabled for longer than three months. Each of her children would qualify for only a $2.50 a week increase in family support. In the meantime, a childless high-income earner would gain $22.50 a week from the tax package.

As Susan St John noted: 'Children's needs are secondary to promoting the work ethic and making dependence on the state a truly miserable experience.' Young children are not interested in whether their parent's lack of income derives from poor pay or from benefits. The need for the basics of life is the same.

Within weeks of the tax cuts, the director of child and family services for the Presbyterian Support Services in Otago, Ian Robertson, said the food banks had never been so busy. In the first month of the tax cuts, one Dunedin food bank gave out an unprecedented 400 parcels, 20 percent more than in the same month the previous year. People needed food, he said, because they had spent their benefits and wages on things like electricity and rent. The *Otago Daily Times* reported that they had also asked for shoes, blankets and clothes to keep their children warm. Most people were paying about 20 percent of their income on electricity. Reverend Robertson's counterpart at the Anglican Methodist family care centre rated July 1996 as the busiest month for two years, with 334 food parcels given out. The Salvation Army's director of community and family services in Dunedin, Captain Annette Garrett, spoke of her concern that 'we've accepted food banks as an institution'.

Poverty in New Zealand is accentuated in winter, and not just in the south of the country. Budget advisors in Northland reported that poor families in the region were going hungry to meet winter expenses. Whangarei Budgeting Service co-ordinator Kaye Tiller told the *Northern Advocate* that people were panicking because they feared power would be cut off when they could not afford to pay their bills. Some families were forced to take extreme measures to try to save money: 'There are families that sit there with the oven door open and elements on because they can't afford other forms of heating.' It is hard to save if you are very poor. Saving money by purchasing specials to put in the freezer ahead of need is simply not an option for many people.

In Dunedin, welfare agencies advised people worried about power bills to pool resources with neighbours and take turns heating up a room for others to come over. Constituents in Christchurch have approached me in anger and fear about Southpower's electricity price increases. People on restricted incomes who were advised to buy nightstore heaters to capitalise on a cheaper night rate have now been hit with an 11.3 percent power price hike. Why 11 percent, when inflation is only 2 percent?

The telephone is taken for granted by most New Zealanders, but remains out of reach for many low-income families. Many cannot afford the line charges, and are forced to share phones. Porirua Budget Service co-ordinator Raewyn Nielsen told the *Dominion* that there are lots of streets in Porirua where a number of families are sharing phones. If a low-income family has a financial problem, the phone is often the first thing to go.

The Kiwi ideal of a lawnmowing, home-owning democracy exists for many, but a large disposed minority without hope is growing. State housing in New Zealand began with the first Labour government. During its term in office from 1935 to 1949 it built more than 32,000 state houses. Rents were based on cost-recovery rather than profit. Tenants were guaranteed security of tenure as long as they lived. These were homes to live and love in.

Labour governments have always given a high priority to housing because the party has recognised that it is one of the most fundamental human needs. Housing is not only necessary to maintain people's physical health. It also provides the base from which activities such as employment, family relationships, education and social participation take place. Without decent housing, a person or family is economically and socially marginalised. Homelessness can, according to UNICEF, be a devastating experience for a child, because 'a home is much more than four walls and a roof. A home provides warmth, security and continuity. Homeless children quickly lose their emotional anchor, and their chance at an education.' With their own home, a family is more likely to stay together. Everyone with a home can remember the thrill and pride of their first home, however modest. That surge of satisfaction is but a bitter dream for many.

Since the 1930s Labour governments have consistently added to the public-housing stock. Public housing has traditionally filled gaps in the supply of low-cost accommodation, building in isolated or commercially undesirable places where there is a social need, not a profit to be made.

It took the National government only five years to demolish one of the best housing systems in the world. They established profit-making companies – called Housing New Zealand and the Housing Corporation – to run state rentals and mortgages. These companies are charging market rents for all state houses and market interest rates for government housing loans. These market moves have been severely criticised by church and community leaders as an attack on the most vulnerable in our society.

National introduced a capped accommodation supplement for renters in public and private housing. The accommodation supplement – or housing voucher – has not covered the full cost of rent increases in state houses, and has forced people either to shift at great personal cost or to make choices between paying for their rent, electricity or food. This voucher approach has done nothing to address the critical problem of housing supply in areas like Auckland. The government has also wound down its involvement in providing mortgage help, and sold mortgages to finance institutions. The most outrageous sale was to Mortgage Corporation, which resulted in low-income families paying the highest interest rates in the country.

National has effectively provided a taxpayer subsidy to landlords in the private sector. It has broken the partnership between central and local government, by charging local authorities market interest rates for loans that were provided for the construction of affordable housing for various groups in the community, including pensioners. Many local authorities are now selling their council housing units. Rents for emergency and community housing have been raised to market levels, causing many such houses to close, and organisations like women's refuges to operate under constant financial stress. They are being forced to spend time raising money for rent, rather than on extending the shelter they provide for those at risk.

The government's housing policies have been a disaster for people on low and modest incomes. State house tenants are now paying more than $485 million to the Government in rents – almost $300 million more than they were in 1992/93. No wonder families are under so much pressure. People can't pay market rents when they are not getting market wages. That's a simple proposition, isn't it?

In my area, there are dozens of empty state houses. It makes absolutely no sense having empty state houses while there are homeless people. The minister then claims there is no need for state housing because empty homes prove there is no demand. Most state house tenants saw their properties as their home. They planted their own gardens, and most painted and kept their homes in excellent condition. They felt they were there for life. Improvements added to their quality of life, not the value of a minister's property portfolio. You can see how streets have become less attractive since the new policy has been introduced. New state houses are only being built for really desperate cases. People of the same backgrounds – frequently single parents, and too often ex-psychiatric patients – are forming little ghettos. Some desperate people won't live on a particular street because that street has a bad reputation. They are then taken off the waiting list because they have turned down a home. Who can blame them for not wanting to go into some suburbs? Taxi drivers often won't go there either. In a twisted form of economic apartheid, the result is that people in desperate straits, frequently same income, same race, same problems, end up grouped together. It's not low-income housing any more, but a ghetto of poor people with desperate problems.

The government has sold off hundreds of state rental houses in Auckland over the last year, and has replaced less than 20 percent of them. As my colleague Phil Goff has pointed out, the reduction in the pool of public rental houses could not be happening at a worse time for low-income families needing to rent homes. The last year has seen the highest-ever population growth in Auckland, putting pressure on the housing market, reducing the availability of homes and pushing up rents. An *Estate* magazine survey in May 1996 revealed that rents in Auckland were 80 to 100 percent higher than in other major cities such as Hamilton and Christchurch, and provincial centres like Rotorua, New Plymouth and Hastings. The government's housing policies have not only made renting a home more costly for low-income families: they have also reduced the availability of lower-income rental homes, forcing families out to the fringes of the city. Worse still, they have destroyed hope. Many people no longer have the expectation of ever having their own home.

Young people require access to decent, affordable housing. In most cases this is provided by their family. Young adults, however, need to be able to establish independent housing. Young people may become homeless if they are forced to leave abusive situations with no financial support or safe refuge in which to live.

Market rents should be scrapped, along with the profit focus of Housing New Zealand. A formula for income-related rents should be reintroduced, with low-income state tenants paying only a quarter of their net incomes in rent. A state house building programme should be establised in areas of high housing demand and need. The government should provide access to subsidised mortages for low and modest income earners, and to others with special housing needs. It should also initiate programmes to help people understand the requirements of home ownership, and investigate alternative programmes to help people own their own home. A community housing division should be set up within the Housing Corporation. It should be responsible for providing appropriate houses to organisations dealing with emergency housing, refuges, services for youth at risk and other groups with special needs.

Young people carry an unfair share of unemployment in New Zealand. They make up 9.7 percent of the working-age population, but represent 40 percent of the unemployed. In their book *Poor New Zealand*, Charles Waldegrave and Rosalyn Coventry wrote that unemployment sets in motion a poverty spiral that 'sucks people down very rapidly, like water emptying out of a bath'.

The real size of the unemployment problem was concealed for the election. Unemployment had dropped by 10,000 since National was elected in 1990, but the number of people on benefits had increased by almost 50,000. In October 1990, the number of registered unemployed was 160,000, or around 7.4 percent of the workforce. After six years of economic recovery based on strong world growth, the registered unemployment figure had fallen to 10,000, or around 6.1 percent of the New Zealand workforce. But there were many more receiving the youth benefit, the 55 Plus benefit, and invalids and sickness benefits.

All told, there are now 360,000 people of working age on the unemployment benefit, the domestic purposes benefit, sickness and invalids' benefits, employment programmes, youth benefits and the 55 Plus benefit.

National slashed the benefits in 1991 because it said it would encourage people to find jobs. All it created was misery, heartbreak and crime. The government failed to explain during the election campaign why there were 25,000 more people on sickness and invalid benefits than in 1990. Is our health system that bad? Instead of going to work, the unemployed are shuffling around from one benefit to the other.

The payment of benefits to those unable to provide for themselves was a cornerstone in the establishment of the welfare state, one of the great achievements of Labour's first administration. But in the years since the passing of the Social Security Act of 1938, the system has been twisted beyond recognition, and it has polarised public thinking.

I am for social *security*. I am opposed to social *welfare*. Norman Kirk once wrote: 'Social security does not imprison people. It sets them free. It does not sap self-reliance. It strengthens confidence by removing fear and insecurity.' Social security, as it was first devised, gave people a chance to get back on their feet , to reclaim control of their lives. It is not a cul-de-sac, but an open road to recovery. Social welfare is a trapdoor to ongoing dependence on the state, a no-exit street to an inferior standard of living. It ought to be a ladder to a better future.

The welfare state is in need of revolution. I do not believe that Michael Joseph Savage, when he instituted the social security system in New Zealand, ever conceived of a day when the sole income of 25 percent of New Zealanders would be from the state through welfare benefits.

Liberation was the intention of the Labour pioneers whose historic legislation built on New Zealand's early moves to care for its people. In the 19th century an assortment of private and public institutions distributed welfare to the needy. Systematic state funding, and the provision of benefits, health and social services, has been a twentieth-century development.

Bismarck introduced the first-ever old-age pension at 60, at a time when only 2.5 percent of the people ever reached the golden age. (By the year 2031, one in every five New Zealanders will be aged over 64, according to Statistics New Zealand.) In New Zealand, means-tested old-age pensions (1898), widows' pensions (1911) and family allowances (1926) were the first steps. Then the widespread poverty and heartbreaking crises that split New Zealand families during the depression of the 1930s illustrated the inadequacy of existing legislation. The Unemployment Act 1930 established a fund to provide limited assistance to unemployed workers.

The first comprehensive social welfare policy was embodied in the Social Security Act, 1938. It replaced the earlier welfare measures, some of which were means-tested, and provided income support and primary health care for everyone in need. New cash benefits included sickness, unemployment, orphans and superannuation (universal at age 65 although later the qualifying age was reduced by Rob Muldoon from 65 to 60). The Family Benefit was extended to include once-excluded groups, such as Asians and illegitimate children. Maoris did not get any benefits until Savage provided equality between the races in the 1930s. The employment tax then in force was replaced by a social security tax and a social security fund was established. This was historic legislation and was built on over the next 50 years with the universal family benefit (1946), supplementary assistance for special needs (1952), and the Domestic Purposes Benefit for single parents (1973).

The crusade by 1960s liberal thinkers for income equality is doomed. The gap between rich and poor is growing. It doesn't matter how many rich there are. We can't have enough rich people. But it does matter how many poor people we have. The unemployment benefit ought to be a temporary situation, not a permanent one. There ought to be a job-search allowance for a couple of months, then a ticket to training and re-skilling toward a permanent job in the private workforce. Alternatively, there should be a permanent job in the community workforce, rebuilding New Zealand's infrastructure, creating something positive in the community whether it be in parks, forests or enhancing our beaches. Another useful option would be military training and upskilling, which could provide some people with a sense of purpose and belonging. An army-trained driver or mechanic is respected by employers ahead of someone from a polytechnic. Why? Because the job is about more than just driving or fixing a truck. It is about character and values – attributes that employers respect.

Progressive Labour people arguing for a revolution in the welfare state are likely to be accused of devouring their own children, of eroding the movement's most basic principles. I disagree. Michael Joseph Savage, Walter Nash and Norman Kirk never regarded the benefits introduced in their times as being a permanent future condition. The dole was temporary, to help people get back on their feet and back into paid work. It was not and should not be regarded as a sole income until retirement and the pension.

In the United States, when President Franklin D. Roosevelt launched a similar welfare state scheme, he warned that, if it became a dependence system, it would be a narcotic to the working classes. Even Karl Marx and the socialist writer/philosopher

Tawney argued that if you do not work you should not get paid. They were primarily talking of the wealthy who did not work, but the argument implicitly applies to the non-working poor.

Of course, most of the poor *do* work. They work hard. They drive our trucks and buses, clean our hospitals and work at night maintaining the essential services. They are the working poor. What has discredited the welfare state is the reality that so many middle- and working-class New Zealanders, struggling to make ends meet on their wages, have friends or know people who do not work because of the imperfections in the welfare state system. They do not work because they can receive more money for not working, which is crazy.

I hear examples of this every week. Middle-aged people are offered work that pays $5 more than the dole. They are not stupid. Human nature being what it is, they do not see any long-term benefit from being in work. What they see is 40 hours of work for an extra $5. They can stay at home and receive almost as much. The working poor see this attitude and it angers them and makes them disillusioned with 'the system'.

The National party's response to this malaise was to cut the benefits, arguing that people would 'pull themselves up by their bootstraps' and go out and get a job. If only it were that simple! There are few jobs, and the Employment Contracts Act has reduced the wages paid for low-income jobs. As a result, the perceived gap between the working and the non-working has disappeared.

All this has brought the system into contempt and built a huge underground 'black economy' where people work, but not on the books. Many tradesmen now offer two prices for their work – a higher price for work that will be declared to Inland Revenue, and a cheaper price for cash under the counter. The country loses millions of dollars in tax revenue each year because of this, and it makes cheats out of good honest workers and employers.

During the 1990 election campaign I was attacked for saying that one of the reasons the country did not create work for people was that it was cheaper to send them the dole by computer, with an electronic deposit in their bank account. This is true. Creating work is more expensive in the short term if you are only looking at the Social Welfare budget. But it is not more expensive if you look at the assets that can be built and the tax that can be gathered from having people in the paid workforce – let alone the rich social dividend paid back when families stay together.

Money put aside for the dole and money for benefits is there to protect the family, or should be. It is money to help keep a family together. The only rationalisation for it can be that every child ought to have a family situation, whatever the shape of that family. Families must have an income – they must not starve. They must have a home, but these supports must not become a permanent way of life. Alas, for too many New Zealanders, they have.

An analysis of beneficiaries on the DPB reveals a vast group of young New Zealanders in danger of becoming prisoners of the welfare system, if they are not already. Young mothers should not become locked away in lonely isolation. We are wasting people we cannot afford to lose. Our young must be encouraged to get a job skill, to be part of the working community, to look forward to a time when, with the children off their hands, they can have the dignity of a job and life outside the welfare circle, and become full citizens in every sense of the word.

To put aside a billion and a half dollars each year to pay a few hundred thousand New Zealanders to do nothing is a short-sighted approach. It should be used in the main to assist businesses to employ people. Simply, it's stupid to tax hard-working New Zealanders and profitable corporations and to then pay others to do nothing when they really want to work. I have never met anybody on the unemployment benefit or the DPB whose ambition was not to get into the workforce and improve themselves. More than anything they want to have some control over their own lives outside a welfare cheque. We define ourselves by our jobs; they are an important part of our identity. The second thing we usually say when we meet a stranger, after asking their name, is: 'What do you do?'

We need a massive redirection of resources and a revolution in our thinking because, quite simply, the present system is not working. This new direction is not meant to be reactive or to punish people for their misfortunes. Rather, it accepts the misfortunes in an understanding way and for a short time helps provide a way out, a launching pad to independence, instead of an economic and social prison.

We have moved beyond the charity state. We introduced accident compensation to provide adequate support to help those who suffered accidents. It was born of the disastrous experiences of the time when, washing our hands of the problem, we allowed lawyers to battle it out with the employers to get whatever compensation they could for their injured clients. Invariably it was guilt money, not compensation, that was paid out. The lawyers got rich. Business suffered. There were big winners in court, but many losers.

New Zealand's ACC system was the best in the world. We enjoyed the best of both worlds – security, fairness and efficiency. Now the contract has been broken. Once we agreed not to sue and businesses agreed to pay for cover. Our new scheme is dearer and provides less cover than our competitors offshore. It will eventually make us less competitive and less secure. It has been so long since the old days of court action that most people have forgotten why there was an agreement between employers, workers and the government to introduce ACC. Expensive litigation costs the United States a fortune. Our system was fairer and cheaper. Now we face the prospect of having the worst of both worlds: no right to sue, and no proper compensation.

Equally with redundancy, a cash 'goodbye' might be nice, but it is not a way out or to the future. The way to the future is permanent, constructive jobs and being part of a society where you can look after yourself and improve your life. Redundancy payments must be channelled into training, skilling and participation in being a full citizen and having the dignity and democratic right to look after yourself and your family in the present, while providing for your future. It is not good enough to have a welfare state that pays people not to be seen, not to be heard and not to participate.

If left alone, the problem will get worse because the Right believes that the unemployed ought to be punished for their sickness or their laziness. There is the attitude that 'they can do better' and a mysterious belief that some invisible hand will distribute jobs among these people. It may be true for those blessed with great talents, or those who chose the right parents, but for the rest of us it is not so. Tough luck and tough future too, unless changes are made that are radical, permanent and real.

Our unemployment problems are of a deep and abiding nature. The real answer is a growing economy that is sustainable, competitive at home and combative abroad. The costs? What are the costs of not doing this? Unemployment is already costing the country $1.4 billion a year, in a nation of 3.4 million people. And there are costs that cannot be put in a Treasury table: the human costs, the costs of violence and insecurity, of broken marriages, of communities torn apart. People need a purpose in life. They need a reason to get up in the morning. The unemployment syndrome of despair and disillusionment is an unacceptable cost, part of a social deficit that is just too expensive.

Treasury gets a lot of stick, much of it deserved. But even they recommended that the government not go ahead with its cruel stand-down provisions for unemployed people waiting for the dole. Losing your job is, after all, bad enough. The government decided that if you lost your job, you should stand down for six months, living off whatever savings you might have and not getting any benefit. The twisted logic was that unemployed people would be encouraged to re-skill themselves and get another job. In the meantime they could live off fresh air and scenery. It was little help to seasonal workers.

In a country where there is an assault every 25 minutes, a robbery every five hours and a burglary every six minutes, the last thing we need is to throw more people on the scrapheap where a resort to crime may be the only way to survive. It is never an excuse, but it is a reality.

What people need is encouragement to keep going, to have another go. You cannot run a country if you decide to have 20 percent of your workforce not working. To put it another way, if you have three million machines in a factory and decide not to have 20 percent of them working, does it make sense to tax the machines that are working to pay for those that are not? Why do we waste people?

It's a particularly stupid situation, yet this is the most profound problem Anglo-American economies face and have yet to solve. I believe the scheme I am putting forward for compulsory work and training will not be easy to establish. All the bureaucrats will fight it, but it must be done. The trouble is that our agencies are tired. Ideas have been tried, but the problems are now so immense that the officials and the advisors are in a state of siege. They have taken shelter in a circle of wagons and now see every new idea as a threat. We need some boldness to break out of that mindset.

No young person must be left to sit on the dole. Every young person should be offered a choice of education, training, employment or community work. Young jobseekers who are at risk of long-term unemployment need to be recognised, so they can receive individual help to ensure they get a job, or continue education or training. Young people should be eligible for employment programmes after three months rather than the current six months. The age at which the full adult minimum wage applies should be lowered from twenty to eighteen, and the minimum youth wage should be raised.

Sally Jackman reminded us in her 1993 report on child poverty in New Zealand, that 'Children are our future, but they are also our present. The way we treat the more vulnerable members of our society, particularly children, people with disabilities and older people, tells us much about our culture.' New Zealand needs a government that cares as much about humans as it does about wild horses. As prominent church members from six denominations pointed out in their recent open letter on poverty, a just society cannot be achieved when individuals pursue what is best for them alone, but only when the community works together for the common good: 'The common good is not what is best for the majority, nor what brings the greatest happiness for the greatest number of people. It is what is best for each and every member of the community.'

There is a dangerous right-wing theory gaining momentum, much of it stolen from the American Republican party by those who watch too much CNN news on Sky television. The theory is that if we cut benefits, people will get jobs. They argue the gap between benefits and wages is too small, and sends out the wrong message: that people are better off not working, so why bother? They are right. But how is it that they never suggest raising wages or lifting the minimum wage? Cutting benefits has not cut poverty: it has increased poverty. It's a bit like the bloke with a headache who takes an aspirin. Then he has another headache and gets more and more angry as he takes more aspirins. Finally he concludes that the aspirins are giving him the headache!

Making the welfare state a springboard and not a depressing, morale-stripping dead-end hammock must be the goal of sane policy-makers.

two

Seeking a New Vision

NEW ZEALAND used to have a health system that was the envy of the world. It was a public, open and free system that guaranteed the highest standards of medical care, irrespective of the patient's wealth. Other countries marvelled at us. They sent experts here to see how the New Zealand model might be adapted to their own countries. Of course we have never had a free health system. You paid every week via your taxes when you were healthy, and paid a small fee to a doctor when you were sick.

But we were pioneers, world beaters. This was the country that in 1907 created the Plunket Society and Karitane hospitals, dedicated to the health and well-being of mothers and infants. The concept of free dental treatment for schoolchildren was introduced in 1921. It was low-tech, decentralised, inexpensive community nursing that worked. For thousands of New Zealand children, a trip to the school dental clinic – the 'murder house' as we so colourfully called it – became as much a part of growing up as jaffas at the Saturday movies and milkshakes. By 1937 New Zealand was able to claim the lowest rate of infant mortality in the world. Progressive politicians boasted of a nation known as Godzone.

But things have gone terribly wrong. New Zealand's health system has headed down the same cul-de-sac as the American health system. It has been restructured on the basis of treating those who can pay, rather than those who need treatment. The irony is that America is now waking up to the reality that a private health system does not work. It is more costly. Good health is good economic policy. Unhealthy children are less likely to learn, more likely to become unemployed and more likely to get into trouble. They are less likely to get their fair share of the New Zealand dream, and more likely to contribute to the New Zealand nightmare.

My parliamentary colleague Annette King has exposed the huge increase in the number of special-needs grants for prescriptions and dental treatment, which shows the unaffordability of health care for people on low incomes. The number of grants for prescription charges for people holding community services cards rose 50 percent in the first five months of 1996. Grants for dental treatment rose 41 percent. The Christchurch Health and Development Study found that children from poor families and children of parents who had left school early tended to use health services less often. The study's executive director, Dr David Fergusson, said: 'The people who are least likely to need the service consume the most of it. The rich get the most of it, and probably get the least benefit because they have the least risk.'

As Sally Jackman points out, children in poor families tend to have relatively poor nutrition, and are consequently more prone to illness and infection. Children who are malnourished do not achieve age-appropriate developmental milestones, even when the malnutrition is mild or moderate. Iron deficiency, which can occur in children not receiving adequate meat and fresh vegetables and in babies being fed cows' milk instead of breast milk, has been identified as a major problem among New Zealand children. The Nutrition Foundation notes that iron is an important factor in maintaining the immune system's ability to prevent and combat infectious agents. It also affects brain function and possibly brain development in the first two years of life.

The foundation recently highlighted what it described as the profound importance of maternal and infant nutrition on the health status of adults. Infant weight, for example, has been related to the incidence of coronary heart disease and insulin resistance. The fatter the baby, the lower the likelihood of coronary heart disease in later life. A plump baby who gains weight well in the first year of life has a heart attack rate one-third that of lower-weight babies. Blood pressure in adults has been shown to be clearly related to infant birth weight and placental size, with a large placenta and low weight being closely associated with increased pressures on the heart during adulthood. The association is even stronger than that linking salt consumption to blood pressure.

Far too many New Zealand children suffer hearing loss through middle-ear infections, which result in what is commonly known as glue ear. Hearing loss occurs more often in winter and has been associated with attending daycare centres. In 1992, 60 percent of all hospitalisations for glue ear were children aged under four. Ethnicity and lower socio-economic status have also been associated with the risk of glue ear, as has passive smoking. The Public Health Commission reported in 1995 that about 10.5 percent of New Zealand children under the age of five suffer from the condition. The hearing test failure rates for Maori children were 13.9 percent, Pacific Island children 14.7 percent and non-Maori children 7.2 percent. The commission noted that although continued ear health education and access to appropriate health services for Maori and Pacific Island children might decrease the failure rate, it is unlikely that the target of 5 percent or less by the year 2000 would be reached. The targets for non-Maori children were, however, considered 'well within reach'. How can children learn with such an impediment? While they wait for medical attention, sometimes up to fourteen months, they slip behind in their schooling. The long-term effects of this could be a lifetime sentence of underachieving. No court would hand down such a cruel sentence.

Lesley Max warned that immunisation of children in New Zealand had fallen to alarming levels, prompting fears of epidemics of certain diseases. She noted that New Zealand levels of polio immunisation were somewhere between 72 and 84 percent, and that Taiwan, with an immunisation level of 80 percent, had experienced a polio epidemic in 1984. Despite an overall decline in vaccine-preventable diseases in New Zealand in recent years, because of immunisations and other factors, the impact of these diseases on health remains significant. And the immunisation coverage for Maori and Pacific Island children is lower than for the rest of the population. Although immunisations are free in New Zealand, families are often too scared to visit their doctor because they owe money from previous visits.

Where is the encouragement, the drive and commitment of health leaders to get families involved?

In late 1994, the medical officer for health in central Auckland, Dr Lester Calder, voiced concerns that increasing poverty in New Zealand might be causing an increase in tuberculosis. 'Given that tuberculosis has been called the barometer of the health of a society, it is cause for concern,' he was quoted in a Press Association report. Dr Calder said that because the highly infectious and often fatal disease was spread in airborne droplets from coughing and sneezing, overcrowding was a big factor in its spread. 'Overcrowding, poor nutrition, delayed access to medical care and diagnoses are all manifestations of poverty and they can certainly be a factor in the spread of disease.' He pointed out that not all those who were infected developed lung disease or other problems associated with tuberculosis. A well-nourished person could develop the disease, but it was more likely in a thin, under-nourished person.

The government must accept some of the blame for what its officials describe as an 'alarming' rate of meningococcal disease in New Zealand. The bacterial infection can cause blood poisoning or damage to the brain. Although prompt treatment with antibiotics can prevent death or permanent disability, close to 400 cases – including 21 deaths – were reported in New Zealand in 1995. Health officials were warning that the number of cases could be even higher in 1996. My colleague Helen Clark drew the link between meningococcal disease and poverty: 'The poorest New Zealanders are paying a heavy price in terms of their children's health because of the government's policies of suppressing benefit and wage incomes, and forcing high housing prices through the commercialisation of state housing.'

Lesley Max noted the lack of paediatric staff in New Zealand, highlighted by Peter Gluckman in his inaugural lecture as professor of paediatrics at Auckland University's School of Medicine in 1988: 'Most sick children present through an emergency room. The very time that they need rapid assessment by a person used to evaluating a sick child and technically skilled to deal with it, they will be seen by someone who almost certainly has had no paediatric experience since his or her undergraduate years. [Auckland] must be the one large city in the world which does not have paediatric staffing of emergency rooms. We can all cite disasters that have resulted.'

As Grant Close, general manager of Auckland's Starship Children's Hospital, has pointed out, some general practitioners are more experienced in managing adult health, and less comfortable with child-health issues. Some childhood diseases, such as meningitis, are extremely difficult to diagnose, but can become very acute within a short period of time. And yet the latest figures I have been able to obtain show that New Zealand has just 117 paediatricians to look after 820,000 children under the age of fifteen. This equates to one paediatrician for every 7006 children. By comparison, the United States has one paediatrician for every 1862 children.

A 1994 report by the Public Health Commission, titled *Our Health – Our Future*, noted that New Zealand had the second worst mortality rate in the OECD for children aged from one to four. Our rate of 52.3 deaths per 100,000 population was exceeded only by Portugal. Three generations ago we boasted the best figures in the world. Forty-two percent of the deaths among New Zealand pre-school children were due to unintentional injuries, and this mortality rate was the highest in the OECD. Almost four out of every ten deaths from unintentional injuries in this age group were caused by motor vehicle crashes. New Zealand's death rate from vehicle crashes was exceeded only by Portugal among OECD countries, and was three times as high as the rate in the United Kingdom and more than 50 percent higher than the rate in Canada.

The ACC, the Land Transport Safety Authority, the Fire Service, police, Plunket and the Office of the Commissioner for Children are to be applauded for their recent joint effort to promote child safety through the Kidsafe Week. The police and Plunket should also be congratulated for their work in encouraging the use of child restraints in cars. In the five years to 1996, 127 children under fourteen were killed as passengers in road crashes, and 41 percent of these youngsters were unrestrained at the time of the crash. One in four infant deaths from unintentional injuries were caused by accidental drowning, and again the New Zealand rate was one of the highest in the OECD. Accidental falls and poisoning by drugs, medicinal substances, and biological substances are other leading causes of hospitalisation of New Zealand infants.

Plunket was founded amid the dismal child health scene at the beginning of this century, when premature and infectious diseases took a huge toll on New Zealand's infants. As many as 25 out of every 1000 babies died from simple diarrhoea. Dunedin doctor Truby King was convinced that New Zealand's high infant mortality rate could be turned around by providing parents with better information and support for rearing children. In 1907 he enlisted the support of prominent Dunedin citizens and formed the Royal New Zealand Society for the Health of Women and Children. His vision was for a health service where local communities would become involved in shaping and delivering the services they needed. Lady Plunket, wife of the then Governor-General, gave her support to the new society, which initially trained nurses, known as Plunket nurses, for work in the community.

The Plunket Society has been the most significant agency with regard to child health in New Zealand. But today it is seriously underfunded, and the cash crisis has forced the closure of family centres in various parts of the country, from Hamilton to Gisborne, New Plymouth and Tauranga. At the time of writing, other centres are under serious threat.

Organisations like Plunket have to battle with four Regional Health Authorities (RHAs) for money. Whereas once Plunket and other health providers used to deal with the Ministry of Health to get funding, they now have to tender contracts to each of the RHAs to win funding for each service they provide. What happens is that these contracts expire at different times. At the time of writing, Plunket has signed contracts with the Southern and Central RHAs, but not with the Midland and Northern RHAs. This makes it impossible for them to do any national planning. By not resourcing existing providers from one funding source, there is also the risk of doubling up on services and throwing those organisations into financial chaos. In Plunket's case there is clear proof that this has already happened.

New Zealand has one of the highest teenage pregnancy rates in the world. UNICEF's 1996 Progress of Nations report ranked New Zealand 33rd out of 44 countries, with a rate of 35 births per 1000 women aged between fifteen and nineteen during the years 1990 and 1995. Countries like Japan, Switzerland, the Netherlands, France and Italy have rates in single figures.

As UNICEF noted, teenage pregnancy has far-reaching consequences both for the mother and child. Mothers face higher risks of complications in childbirth and their infants are at greater risk of premature birth, low birthweight, death in the first year of life, and having developmental problems. Becoming pregnant at too young an age affects a young women's own development, limiting education and lifestyle opportunities. For the infants born to teenage mothers, the years of early childhood may be marked by poverty, poor care, and instability, which helps to perpetuate problems from one generation to the next.

Kawerau gained some unwelcome publicity in May 1996 when it was revealed that the Bay of Plenty town had a teenage pregnancy rate two and a half times as high as the national average. Live births per 1000 women aged between fifteen and nineteen totalled 89, compared with the national average of 35. Dr Ian Gourlay, of the Tarawera Medical Centre, told the *New Zealand Herald* that high unemployment, high dependence on benefits, low economic status, limited opportunities and low self-esteem all contributed to the town's unenviable statistic. He also noted that the teenage pregnancy rate was highest among the town's unemployed Maori women. Kawerau's Tuwharetoa Ki Kawerau Haurora Trust has opened a clinic to provide family planning and sexual health education, as well as counselling and advice for the town's youth. Trust manager Adelaide Waata says some of the young women are embarrassed to talk about sexual health issues, and others felt uncomfortable in a general-practice environment.

Political correctness has stood in the way of vital public education on the dangers of teenage pregnancy. When asked why there was no public education on the matter, child psychiatrist Dr Karen Zelas told Lesley Max: 'It's very difficult to speak out on that. It's just politically uncomfortable, because you're made to appear anti-feminist.' A similar response came from Julia Mendelssohn, programme director with the Family Development and Support Directorate in the Department of Social Welfare, who said: 'You're getting into sticky issues, issues of human rights and state intervention. There's no law that says you can't have a baby.' Lesley Max concluded that the Department of Social Welfare had 'paralysed itself with gender and cultural sensitivity'.

In an election year, Health Minister Jenny Shipley announced a five-year strategy on sexual and reproductive health. The goals include better information about the inter-relationships between reproductive health and sexual health, education, employment and family life, and improved access to contraceptive information and products. This is a good start.

The five-year strategy also aims at reducing New Zealand's rising abortion rate. Recent cases of protesters being arrested outside hospitals where abortions are being performed highlight the need for a review of our privacy and trespass laws. Women who lawfully seek abortions should be entitled to absolute privacy. People opposed to abortion are entitled to their views, and entitled to protest. But they are not entitled to harass, embarrass and intimidate women who have just made one of the most difficult decisions they can make.

A national alcohol survey by the Alcohol and Public Health Research Unit at the University of Auckland revealed further disturbing statistics for the young people. Almost one in four males between the ages of 18 and 24 consumed large quantities of alcohol at least once a week, and 70 percent consumed large quantities at least once a month. One in five females aged between 16 and 24 consumed large quantities at least once a week, and just under half at least once a month.

Almost one in three young male drinkers reported that they felt drunk at least once a week. One in seven 16- to 24-year-olds felt their drinking was having a large or medium harmful effect on their financial position. Just over 30 percent of young people aged between fourteen and nineteen told researchers that they had drunk alcohol at hotels in the previous twelve months, and almost four out of ten had purchased takeaway alcohol in the previous twelve months. More than a quarter of young women had been sexually harassed by someone who had been drinking, and 22 percent of young males and 12 percent of young women had been assaulted by drinkers over the previous twelve months.

The contribution of alcohol to New Zealand's horrendous road toll, and the tragic over-representation of young people in the statistics, have been well documented elsewhere. Much comes down to attitudes. Lesley Max highlighted the difference in attitudes between Sweden and New Zealand: 'In Sweden, one would face ostracism for behaviour that is perfectly acceptable in New Zealand in the same socio-economic grouping. The judicial system, the officially punitive system, works alongside the social system and reinforces it, but it cannot be a substitute for it. Attitude is all.'

It has been estimated that as many as 3500 New Zealand children could be born each year with severe mental and physical defects caused by their mothers drinking alcohol during pregnancy. Recent studies suggest that as many as four out of ten New Zealand mothers continue to drink while they are pregnant.

Foetal alcohol syndrome is considered one of the leading causes of mental retardation in the Western world. A pregnant woman can cause serious complications for her foetus by drinking about three standard drinks a day, according to Gregg Duester of the La Jolla Cancer Research Foundation in California. Dr Duester told a seminar at Massey University in 1994 that initial symptoms of foetal alcohol syndrome include deformities of the eyes, mouth, and nose at birth, followed by mental retardation, slow learning and problems at school. Foetal damage occurs primarily in the first eight weeks following conception, at a time when many women do not know they are pregnant. The United States has embarked on a campaign to label liquor containers with a warning to pregnant women that the contents could harm the unborn child. Some states require warning signs to be displayed at liquor outlets.

The number of New Zealand mothers who smoke tobacco during pregnancy is also alarming. Smoking has become one of the most contentious health issues in New Zealand. Helen Clark's moves to cut nationwide smoking levels attracted considerable flak when she was Minister of Health, but she was right.

About one woman in three smokes during pregnancy, but the proportion is higher among Maori women: an alarming 68 percent. Smoking during pregnancy has been linked to a range of childhood ailments, from cot death to glue ear, bronchitis and pneumonia. The risk of cot death is four to five times as high for infants whose mothers smoke and regularly share their bed with their child, compared with infants of mothers who neither smoke nor share the bed. As many as a third of cases of glue ear can be attributed to exposure to tobacco smoke.

It has been estimated that unless the current uptake of smoking decreases, nearly 60,000 New Zealanders now under the age of twenty can be expected to die early from smoking.

One in every ten of our children have tried marijuana before they are fourteen. Some are being suspended from school for using and selling drugs. It sounds like New York, but it is the reality of New Zealand in 1996. All the problems associated with the sick societies of North America and Europe are coming to our country. Police statistics reveal that more than 6000 school-age children have been caught for cannabis offences since 1990. Of that number, 1158 were aged between fourteen and sixteen, 124 aged between ten and thirteen, and three were under nine. As my colleague George Hawkins says, the figures are just the tip of the iceberg. Many more thousands of children are using cannabis, but not coming into contact with the police.

There is a strange liberal malaise about drug use in New Zealand. The danger signs have been there for years, but it is difficult to convince the media that there is a problem. The government is sending out mixed signals about drug use. The taxpayer will spend $3 million on a media campaign to stop cigarette smoking, but will not spend one cent on a similar campaign on drug use. Pressure groups are rightly vocal about the advertising of alcohol and cigarettes, but strangely silent about the use of other drugs, no doubt because such opposition would be considered politically incorrect. The 'flower children' of the 1960s – now in their middle-aged years – dominate the government, the media and the pressure groups.

Trevor Grice, the director of the Life Education Trust, has been campaigning against drugs for years. He has built up a fleet of twenty education trucks that now visit half the schools in the country. He receives not one cent from the government.

The drug culture gives comfort to those who feel hopeless and unwanted, and think life has little future. With youth unemployment at more than 50 percent, there is no shortage of people vulnerable to drugs. Drug farms and factories in some parts of New Zealand are probably the biggest industry outside tourism and horticulture. This sub-culture has been captured by gangs and a mutant strain of Maoridom that accepts drugs and violence as the normal way of life. There has been a perversion of Maori culture. Young men wearing filthy clothes and obscene and historically inappropriate tattoos are seeking to justify the taking and selling of drugs through claiming some sort of perverted Maori warrior status. That is nonsense. It is poisoning the young, degrading the participants and dividing and frightening the community. I've been to countries where cannabis has been used for generations, societies like Morocco, and the impact on people is appalling.

Some parts of New Zealand, such as Northland, have developed a sub-culture of drugs and fear. The drug world is corrupting civil society. Children are going to school dazed and dopey as passive cannabis smokers. Cannabis lowers the IQ and impairs judgment. If these kids were drinking a bottle of gin a day the authorities would act.

At a recent seminar I attended in Melbourne, respected researchers said that marijuana should be regarded as a hard drug rather than a soft one, and was far too dangerous to be made legal. Professor Fred Goodwin of the George Washington University in Washington DC said research showed that any analogy between the use of marijuana and alcohol was difficult to support. 'There is very little argument that daily use of marijuana has an effect, but for the 70 percent of people who are social drinkers, daily use is not harmful.'

He explained that one of the great difficulties with marijuana was that the active ingredient THC metabolised slowly, while alcohol passed through the body relatively quickly. 'With THC you can find measurable quantities (in the body) four days later, which causes a "staircasing" effect of piling up more and more of the chemical if it is used one day after another.' It affects children and adolescents more than adults. There needs to be a public media campaign to make drug-taking less romantic and to take the health issue more seriously.

Twenty-five years ago the American singer Dean Martin had his own television show. One of his gimmicks was to sing and tell jokes with a cigarette in one hand and martini in the other. Sometimes he would slip off the piano, acting – or maybe not acting – drunk. A quarter of a century ago such behaviour was considered funny. It wouldn't be today. Yet we now have television shows glorifying people, like Jim in the television series *Taxi*, who appear dopey with cannabis or brain-damaged through drug overuse. Attitudes will change. They had better, because they are dangerous. Have you ever noticed how people who smoke or drink know they are being stupid? They know it is killing them. But cannabis smokers get very agitated and indignant when challenged. Their ultimate defence is that 'cannabis is no worse than cigarettes or alcohol'.

Last century Maori leaders cursed Europeans for almost destroying the Maori race by introducing alcohol,VD and influenza. Within a generation, their great-great-grandchildren will stand on maraes and curse those who stood by and watched young Maori destroy their lives with drugs. I was shocked recently when a member of the New Zealand Maori Council called for the legalisation of cannabis. How can parents say 'no' to drugs and protect their children if their leaders cave in to political correctness instead of leading by example? Some have claimed gangs won't sell cannabis if it is legalised. Why not? Legalising or decriminalising the drug will simply mean they can sell it at the school gate rather than behind the bike sheds. We now have third-generation drug addicts. We have failed them, and they will punish us. New Zealand will pay for it, one way or another.

Young people with drug addictions are being refused methadone treatment. That is cruel, inhuman and short-sighted. Telling addicts to wait for treatment is like asking a pregnant women to wait twelve months to see a doctor. Addicts do desperate and dangerous things to maintain their habits. They sell drugs, which increases the problem. Many steal. Others resort to prostitution, risking exposure to AIDS and other sexually transmitted diseases. Families are torn apart. Non-treatment causes pain and suffering to individuals, but it is also a threat to ordinary people whose property and health is at risk. Seventy percent of addicts have hepatitis C. They are infected time bombs who deserve better.

The Southern RHA has a particularly poor record in its treatment of drug addicts. In answer to a parliamentary question, the Minister of Health revealed that the average length of time on a waiting list for treatment in the Southern RHA was 75.6 weeks. North Health was next with a sixteen-week wait. A person in Christchurch must wait almost five times as long as a person in Auckland.

Schemes exist to help young victims of drug abuse. Early intervention does work. Papanui High School, in my electorate, runs classes in a church hall across the road. But the schemes receive little financial assistance. They fall between government-funding cracks because they involve several departments, such as health, welfare, justice, police and Maori affairs. We can't just continue to turn thousands of kids out of school and our backs on the problem, because a few years down the track it will cost $50,000 a year to keep each one of them in prison.

Children too young to buy cigarettes legally, or drive a car, cannot be arrested by the police for glue sniffing. If a young person is sitting in a shop doorway with a bottle of vodka, or even a packet of cigarettes, the police can do something about it. But they cannot confiscate commercial products available at many hardware shops and petrol stations. I have been told of a service station that was selling petrol to children in empty coke bottles at 50 cents each. In Dunedin, the police have found children as young as eleven sniffing potentially fatal butane gas, lighter fluid, LPG and some fly sprays. Christchurch doctor Sue Bagshaw told *The Press* that young people are caught in a vicious circle. Many can see no way out other than the temporary escape gained in being drunk or stoned. The system also works against young people, many of whom are unable to find work, but also are too young to get a benefit, and no longer welcome at home.

Anxiety disorders are the most common mental-health problems affecting young people. The way we treat disturbed young people is a national disgrace and a cause for great shame. New Zealand's mental-health programmes are in crisis. We are not alone: this is the experience of all liberal, democratic societies. The care of acutely disturbed psychiatric patients outside hospitals, in what is dishonestly called 'the community', has not worked. It has been discredited internationally as a failed experiment. After tragic cases of murder, rape, suicide and terror, these policies are being re-thought. Reports of inquiries from the United Kingdom and United States point out the shortcomings of existing policies.

Mental health was the first example of socialised health care. Even in medieval times, society recognised that the individual could not cope. Nor could individual families, churches and monasteries provide a common answer and service. At London's Bedlam Hospital, people paid to rattle the cages and look and laugh at the afflicted. People were once locked away for minor problems. Most were better off out of the gothic, Dickensian-style institutions that dominated psychiatric medicine. Asylums, which were created to provide safe havens, places of peace and care, had become prisons for many.

New Zealanders who had been in places like Oakley, Sunnyside, even Templeton Hospital – sometimes for over 40 years – have found a better, more fulfilling life in the care of the community. Community values and the stigma, shame and embarrassment have thankfully changed. Perhaps 80 percent of patients are better off, but not all.

In response to the cruel and frequently wrongful imprisonment of the mentally disturbed from the 1950s to the 70s, New Zealand followed the fashion to move decisively from institutional care to community care. All institutional care was suddenly deemed bad; all community care was good. The wonder drugs of the 1950s were also seen as a cure. Anti-depressants would cure the dangerously depressed. Tranquillisers would save the severely schizophrenic, just as surely as penicillin killed pneumococci. Medication was the golden bullet that would effect 'cures.' The reality that patients might not take medication away from the stern control of hospitals was ignored.

Thomas Szasz, an American psychiatrist and best-selling author, argued that mental illness was not actually illness at all. It was an early example of political correctness winning over common sense and common experiences. Institutional care was seen as some eighteenth-century witchhunt, rather than a humane branch of medical care. Michael Foucault in France led the intellectual debate, explaining that institutional care was a repressive appparatus of the bourgeois state. Insitutionalism was inherently repressive, and when the acutely disturbed and deluded committed offences they should be treated like any other criminal.

Contracting out and so-called 'community care' have come together in New Zealand and conspired to create a disaster. We have closed down hospitals, reduced bed and ward numbers, and are now planning to rebuild similar wards inside prisons.

The 'market' view of mental health is partly based on the so-called 'rights of the individual'. 'The right to be crazy', it is called in serious publications. The right to be eccentric, different and inappropriate. They say you have the right to live your own life, without the state or society telling you how to live. Even if you are burning yourself, taking drugs, or causing pain and terrorising your family and community. It is individualism gone crazy. The Privacy and Human Rights Acts, and mental health legislation, give all rights to the disturbed and no value to the rights of families or responsibilities of society. It is a cowardly cop-out. It is society's moral responsibility to intervene and stop the pain.

Too often, desperately sick people are released without backup, against medical advice and the wishes of their family, only to go into psychotic episodes that have resulted in murder, rape and suicide. Unspeakably cruel and tragic examples of molestation and families being terrorised do not seem to concern the 'know-all' health bureaucrats and health politicians. Mothers who have been beaten by their children and have seen them offend against innocents cry out for help. We no longer have patients: they are 'clients' – another dishonest, politically correct description.

The Privacy Act and commercial confidentiality arguments are being used to cover up the grim reality of a tragic truth. We have got it wrong. In the United Kingdom and Australia, the system is under the spotlight for the same reasons. Care in the community is not working for many, and it is getting worse. It is putting extra strain on the few beds for the acutely disturbed, and soon more horror stories will hit the media, telling of parents who have given up on their children. Or children who have been brutalised or will brutalise them.

British reports I have read sound depressingly familiar:

families terrorised, services underfunded and overlapping, with patients missing out. Politicians responding to headlines, then letting the issue sleep until the next crisis and tragedy. In New Zealand, the government will give more money to mental health because of recent 'bad' publicity. They know they are losing votes. Their answer will be more bureaucracy and more patient visits by social workers, as if these patients have not suffered enough. That will not work either. The chronic shortage of beds and institutions has created a nightmare for families, the police, patients and GPs. Psychiatric wards once offered shelter to the distressed and deluded. Such people should not have to prove they are seriously disturbed, or hurt themselves or others in order to get a place of peace, so they can get some purpose back in their lives.

In late 1995, a sixteen-year-old Christchurch youth spent a week in a windowless police cell because authorities did not know what to do with him. It was barbaric and surely must have breached every international treaty and convention on the treatment of the sick. He had been arrested after an incident in which his desperate parents had tried to stop him committing suicide. The police were left in an impossible position. They hate having to be the only 24-hour service for the disturbed.

One sick, sad young soul was refused treatment at Sunnyside Hospital. He walked across Christchurch in his bare feet until they bled. The police picked him up when he was discovered naked in a park with a broomstick up his rectum. He was again sent home. He killed his father and later himself. Who are the real criminals here?

Another tragic case involved a 21-year-old Massey man with a mental age of five who was turned loose by the courts to sleep on the streets because there was nowhere else to send him. The man, who had stolen a three-dollar chocolate bar, had spent ten days in prison. His lawyer warned that if the court let him go, he would be a danger to himself and the public. He had previously spent time in Lake Alice mental hospital for sex attacks, and there was a danger he would regress into this behaviour if not under proper supervision. The lawyer told the court that the man had impulsive violent outbursts, and in the past had accosted young girls and stolen women's underwear. The judge couldn't provide any help. If the man had raped he would have got care – but in prison.

In May 1996, a Wellington judge sentenced two dangerous schizophrenics to jail so they could receive their treatment. One had stabbed a woman when he attempted to steal her handbag; the other had robbed someone at knifepoint. Such cases are becoming all too familiar. We let people out of hospitals. They stop taking their medication. Someone is assaulted, stabbed or worse. The only secure psychiatric care we offer is inside prisons.

I wrote a private bill to force the government into a public inquiry into mental health and how it affected young people. I had the numbers in Parliament and the government agreed to set up the Mason Inquiry. It seemed like progress. It did not go far enough, and then the government double-crossed Judge Mason and so weakened the report that this respected judge felt compelled to go public and distance himself from the government's policy response. Jim Crowe, a member of the Mason committee, refused a highly paid advisory job on National's Mental Health Commission, calling it 'a toothless tiger'. I was also conned. I should have known better.

New Zealand is now one of the most dangerous places in the world for disturbed young suicidal males. The government has turned a blind eye to youth suicide, because the problem is just too big for it to handle. Between 1991 and 1993, 40 out of every 100,000 young New Zealand males took their own life, according to UNICEF's Progress of Nations report. Only the Russian Federation and Lithuania had worse rates. New Zealand's rate was close to twice that of the United States, Canada, Ireland and Austria, more than three times that of the United Kingdom and Germany, and four times that of Sweden, Japan and the Netherlands. The New Zealand rate is almost certainly higher, because our coroners do not call a death 'suicide' unless a person's intention to kill him or herself is beyond doubt. Traffic accidents, for instance, can sometimes be a cover for suicide.

According to Dr Rob McGee of Otago Medical School, the strongest predictor of suicidal thoughts at the age of fifteen is a feeling of detachment from parents. His finding was based on the results of a study of development among 1000 young people from birth to the age of 21. Adolescents who talked about suicide also used drugs or alcohol to make themselves feel better, he told the *Dominion* in 1994. 'Most kids experiment with alcohol in the context of friends at parties and so on. But a significant number of these kids were actually using alcohol and drugs as a way of dealing with depression.'

Other factors which have been linked to youth suicide include deteriorating academic performance, exposure to suicidal models in the media, and unemployment. Redundancy and other social changes have hit young New Zealand men particularly hard, since males tend to be 'defined' by their jobs. Youthline co-ordinator Lewis Brown points out that New Zealand teenagers tend to keep their emotions bottled up. As a result of not finding outlets for their emotions, they get into risk-taking behaviour, such as 'drinking and driving and getting stoned off their faces'. He told the *Evening Post*: 'As a nation, we have poor communication skills, a do-it-yourself mentality. Young men have to be seen to be strong. There's a real underlying New Zealand value that you don't talk about problems.'

Male depression has always been a taboo subject in New Zealand. There are nowhere near as many male support groups and action groups as there are for women. Women have been better advocates, and good on them. They have done a superb job in lobbying and publicising women's health issues. It is time men copied some of their successful techniques.

Improving the health of New Zealand's children and young people is of the utmost priority. It is the most basic human right. Truby King was a visionary who thought laterally, beyond the narrow confines of institutions. We need visionaries like him again, to look out across the next 50 years and see ways to preserve and enhance the health of New Zealand's children. We need to advance the Plunket system and marry it to today's high technology.

Why can't we have a daily Plunket programme on television, to teach parents the latest in child-caring techniques? We have the tradition of the police on the beat in the community. Why not have Plunket nurses out and about with mobile phones, so mothers watching a specialised television programme on child-rearing can phone their community nurse to come around and provide further advice? Let's be pioneers again, innovate, take risks and lead.

Raising the standard of living of families on low incomes is a critical element in the mix. We can begin by raising benefit and family support levels, reducing taxes for low-income earners, and reinstating income-related rents for state house tenants. Home-based health visits should be provided for all mothers of newborn babies. Funding for agencies providing such services, like Plunket and Tipa Ora, should be boosted, so that the number of home visits a child receives in their first five years can be increased. Plunket must be properly funded from a single source. In the first five years of a child's life, it is vital that families should have access to healthcare services without having to worry about whether they can afford them. No child under five should have to pay to go to the doctor. Prescriptions can also be a major expense for families with young children. Standard charges for prescriptions should be removed immediately for children under five, and charges for older children should be reduced.

District health services should work with schools to identify the immediate need for school food, or other programmes, to improve child nutrition. Parent-support services should be offered to families who are identified as being under serious stress. These services should provide ongoing home support tailored to the specific needs of the family. We also need family care services that offer community-based advice and support to families with older children. The aim should be to prevent problems occurring which would put the health and well-being of the children at risk.

Community care need not mean a cold, damp bedsit or boarding house. And institutional care need not be an overcrowded ward, as popularised by Ken Kesey's best-selling book and movie *One Flew Over the Cuckoo's Nest*. We need to create decent shelters, places of peace and tranquility for those who cannot cope or look after themselves. The word 'asylum' need not be a menacing word or signify a place that cruelly represses people.

We need to ensure that resources are available for the full range of mental services, including inpatient and acute, sub-acute and extended care accommodation, as well as community-based support for patients and caregivers, counselling and referral services and crisis intervention services. The development of intensive-care community teams has helped relieve some of the pressure on district psychiatric nurses, so we should continue to fund these initiatives. No mental health patient should be discharged into community care before appropriate services have been put into place for them. Any district health service that is considering discharging such a patient should be required to ensure an agreed care plan has first been developed.

I feel passionately about preserving the public health system in New Zealand, which is probably not surprising since it saved my life. I successfully underwent treatment for cancer in 1979, with a new type of chemotherapy that was enormously expensive at the time. I was grateful to the taxpayer and the welfare state, because I could never have afforded it otherwise. Yet without that treatment I would have died. Doctors once gave me a lifespan measured in months.

It is just unbearable to see two nations develop in New Zealand – one that can buy good health, and one that cannot. Knowing the strengths and successes of our health system, and knowing that it can work and save the lives of people who could not otherwise afford expensive treatment, I could not possibly support its privatisation. The lesson in child health is to learn from our great-grandparents. They were not all wrong.

three

The Learning Deficit

> The skill, dexterity and knowledge of a nation's people is the most powerful engine of its economic growth.
>
> – Adam Smith, *The Wealth of Nations*

UNTIL RECENTLY, New Zealanders prided themselves on the quality of their education system. It was a system evolved from the pioneer days when settlements were isolated and schooling was often left to the churches or a mix of private and public organisations. Education nominally came under the provincial councils, when the provinces were established in 1852, but there was no degree of uniformity, nor were there standards of efficiency. Neither was the need for education properly appreciated by the population. In 1876 only half of the children in New Zealand between five and fifteen were attending school at all. A free, secular and compulsory education system was embodied in the Education Act of 1877.

Today, school attendance is compulsory for children between the ages of six and sixteen, with almost all children beginning primary school on their fifth birthday. The benefits of a good education are self evident and, unlike the slapdash approach in 1876, most parents today are clearly trying to give their offspring the best possible start at life. The boom in early childhood education is proof of this. In the past twenty years, attendance at early childhood centres around the country has nearly tripled. Statistics like this hearten me.

I'm proud that the fourth Labour government gave top priority to the early childhood area. Overseas research has proven the value of harnessing young minds early in life. Giving a child a good start is so critical for a life in which education and skills determine living standards.

Labour has always been the education party. Peter Fraser, Labour's first Education Minister, said that children were the most important asset of the nation and that wise expenditure on education constituted the most important social investment the state could make, retaining in the long run its richest dividends. Education was seen as the way of breaking the cycle of poverty. It was an individual good, but it was also a social and economic good. A nation that restricted opportunity worked against its own wider and long-term economic interests. Elitism in edu-cation restricted a nation's growth. Equal opportunity meant enfranchising all its citizens. The British disease of class meant that the doctors, engineers and leaders came from the same areas and gene pool, and helped bring that nation to its knees by becoming less innovative and competitive. Labour has always recognised the need to make successful taxpayers and contributors from all social backgrounds regardless of gender and race. Equality is good in itself, but it also makes good economic sense.

We are seeing the emergence of rich and poor schools. Cost-cutting has stretched resources and compromised the quality of early childhood education. Parents are worried that standards of education and discipline are seriously slipping. They feel their children are not receiving the quality education that was available to them during their own school years.

Finding extra money to pay for school activities is an increasing worry for families on low incomes. Schools are being extended beyond their role as educators to cope with increasing social pressures. Tertiary students are incurring crippling debts at universities, polytechnics and training institutions. Lack of funding is severely eroding the quality of education in rural areas and for children with special needs. And Maori educational achievement remains a national disgrace.

Economies that don't operate on the basis of utilising all the talents of their people in the end handicap themselves. You can't run a football team or a nation if you lock out half the potential participants because they are female, from a poor background, or the wrong colour.

UNICEF talks about the need to harness enlightened self-interest. Business leaders in countries like the United States, United Kingdom and New Zealand 'are beginning to realise that the swelling tide of child neglect has potentially disastrous consequences not only for the individual child, but for society as a whole. Deprived, undereducated children grow into problem-ridden youngsters who are extremely difficult to absorb into the modern workforce . . . The skill needs of advanced industrial economies are moving rapidly up the scale, with most new jobs demanding more education and higher levels of language, maths and reasoning skills. Qualifications for jobs, even low-wage jobs, are rising. Estimates are that by the late 1990s, the average job will require a full year more education than was true in the 1980s.'

A nation's wealth is no longer based on steel, coal or oil. This is the post-industrial age. It is the information age. Competitive advantage is now based on education and skills. New Zealand is slipping behind internationally. Children in our major competing marketplaces are better educated, stay at school longer and leave with higher qualifications than comparable students in New Zealand. In many cases, they are also more likely to get a job than the New Zealand school leaver, and later to enjoy a higher standard of living. To compete with these people we must meet or better their standards. If we don't win this battle, we will perish. We will become the white and brown trash of the Pacific Basin.

The book *Children: Endangered Species?* noted the conditions in one New Zealand school: 'Many of the parents are not literate in any language. Thirty-three percent of the children come from single-parent families. Thirty-eight percent of the families are supported by a benefit. Some homes house up to sixteen people. Half the new entrants have had no pre-school experience. One in five has toileting problems, reflecting emotional trauma as well as a lack of pre-schooling. Head lice, scabies and ear troubles are very common. The staff deal with cases of physical and sexual abuse. Some 10 percent of the children are markedly unstable, while others display symptoms of anxiety. Some are violent. Many of the children are poorly clothed. Many come to school without lunch and may "scab" for food. Some are malnourished.'

Sally Jackman notes that children's educational opportunities are being limited by their families' financial circumstances, and by the level of poverty in their communities: 'The causes of educational under-performance are complex and cannot be explained by reference to financial considerations alone. It is clear, however, that schools are putting time and money into dealing with children's basic needs.' A University of Canterbury study of Canterbury schools in 1992 and 1993 recorded increasing inequality between schools since 1990, and noted large differences in the ability of schools to collect fees and raise funds in their communities.

The Christchurch Health and Development Study found that although 95 percent of children received some form of pre-school education, children from disadvantaged families did not arrive until they were aged four and a half, while advantaged children did so at two or three. Not surprisingly, a survey by the New Zealand Council for Educational Research in 1991 found that the best resourced schools were in middle-class areas, with mainly Pakeha populations. Some schools are having to choose between providing breakfasts or library books for their pupils. This often has little to do with lack of parental organisation or motivation. One school I visited was overwhelmed by poor parents wanting to help out. There were so many, they got in the way. The school had to turn some parents away and enforce a roster scheme for helpers.

Socio-economic status is also reflected in exam results. The state secondary schools that recorded the highest marks in Bursary last year were located predominantly in high-income communities. The poorest-performing schools were predominantly in low-income areas. Canterbury and Victoria University academics David Hughes and Hugh Lauder have written about the waste of talent caused by the failure of talented young people to succeed at school. They surveyed more than 2700 school leavers and found that students of high abilities from lower socio-economic backgrounds were substantially less successful at school than equally talented children from more privileged families.

Most teachers, parents and experts will say that Tomorrow's Schools was a good concept. It was rushed through, with not enough space for people to keep up and plan, which was typical of Labour's reforms. But no one wants to go back to the old system. Giving more power to parents through bulk funding was, on the surface, a good principle. However, the result is that richer areas do better than poorer areas and 'white flight' – where Pakeha parents shift their children to what they perceive as better schools – becomes common. At great sacrifice, many poor and middle-income parents now send their children to church and private schools. Why? The traditional response of the Left is to accuse them of snobbery. That's not altogether true or fair. I know of parents who are keeping their families poor by dedicating the low income of one partner just to give what they see as a better chance for their children in a private school. The cash race is on. How do parents keep up when children are asked to bring to school more and more money for school projects, trips or basic needs?

Schools in Auckland have broken the law by refusing new entrants. They have no choice, such is the overcrowding and lack of resources. When a headmaster – a public servant – does this, they put their job, promotions and opportunities for the future on the line. Despite the claim of 'open opportunity' for students to go to any school, 40 percent of Auckland's secondary schools have restrictive enrolment schemes. More than 17 percent of primary and intermediate schools nationwide operate restrictive regions. Schools and pupils are paying the price for bad planning. Only a few years ago the government paid you to train as a teacher; now you must pay them. The result is that New Zealand is importing mature teachers from Scotland and Australia, while our own ambitious students are turned away.

If anyone needed convincing of the depths to which educational standards have sunk for some children, or of the existence of two nations in this country, it came in the form of an Education Review Office report which revealed that 80 percent of students in at least two New Zealand schools were 'functionally illiterate'.

Research by the University of Canterbury's speech and language therapy programme exposed the grim fact that 17 percent of five-year-olds in their first four months at Christchurch schools were not ready to start normal pre-reading activities, because of speech/language problems. That's almost one in five children with a significant speech/language problem. Kate McNabb, a therapist with the Special Education Service, explained that these children lacked the ability to understand spoken language and had difficulty managing normal language instructions. Children with poor speech fall behind and are at risk of severe and persistent literacy problems. The Special Education Service believes that speech/language problems are very common and misunder-stood. This could be the biggest hidden disability in New Zealand.

The Reading Recovery programme pioneered by Dame Marie Clay has undoubtedly changed the lives of thousands of New Zealand youngsters who would otherwise have fallen through the cracks. The programme takes children out of the classroom for half an hour a day for individual teaching, which enables them to progress at their own pace. Reading Recovery was introduced in the late 1970s, and given permanent status by the Labour government in 1984. The programme has been so successful that it is now being used in countries such as Australia and the United States.

Lesley Max found that reading recovery is not available for many children. For some, the programme is curtailed before the need is fully met, or withdrawn because of a child's poor attendance record. If a reading-recovery teacher leaves a school, the programme can be terminated for up to two years until a replacement teacher can be trained. And the programme is not available at many rural schools. Lesley Max notes that parents can be surer that their child will receive appropriate dental care at school than they can be that their child will emerge a fully competent reader. Research has also indicated that some children who make advances while on reading recovery programmes fall behind again once they return to regular reading classes.

Thanks to the vision of author Alan Duff and his Books in Homes initiative, an estimated 180,000 books have been distributed to tens of thousands of underprivileged New Zealand children. As Duff told *North and South* magazine, 'If you don't read, you're lost, trapped in a dreary cycle of illiteracy, poverty, anger and violence.' The government has now backed the project, with a one-off grant of $250,000.

Lesley Max points to studies in Britain, the United States and New Zealand that demonstrate marked differences between the pattern of language in upper/middle-class homes and in lower-class homes. 'The former tend to demonstrate a complex and rich language structure, while the latter demonstrate much curter, briefer, less elaborate utterances and are, as they relate to children, much more authoritarian. The child who goes to school after spending his or her first five years in the former kind of home starts school with a much greater ability to comprehend and process the messages that come his or her way, and a more positive attitude towards problem-solving and a greater readiness to read. The child who has grown up without the use of language to make his or her world comprehensible and predictable adds a greater degree of anxiety to his or her other comparative disadvantages, and anxiety is an obstruction to learning.'

In a recent column in the *Dominion*, Nelson writer Agnes-Mary Brooke noted that language once regarded as offensive is in common use: 'Too many of our ill-spoken young sound more like the products of a semi-literate frontier society than one where the hard-won, civilising customs of the past are valued, and passed on.'

Mrs McCormack taught me, my elder and younger brothers. There are fifteen years between us. Now pupils in some areas are lucky if they have the same teacher for a year. The school as a place of stability no longer exists for many. Schools are finding it harder to get relieving teachers. This is a nationwide problem; it is not restricted to the usual 'hard-to-staff' areas. Schools in Auckland's eastern, western and southern suburbs, Rotorua, Taupo, Taranaki, Christchurch and the West Coast have gone to the press recently to report their anxiety about the relief-teacher shortage. One school last year had a pool of fifteen relievers on which to call daily. It now has one reliever who is only available two days a week, one who has a baby under six months old and can do only the odd day, and one who is older than 65 and can relieve for half a day if the school is absolutely stuck. This is just one example of the type of pressure schools are under.

Poor pay, lack of respect and disillusionment are causing

teachers to leave the profession, and the shortage of full-time teachers has meant relief teaching pools have been depleted.

The teachers are trying their best. In poorer areas it is the teachers who are always putting their hands in their pockets. They are the ones who run the food kitchens. And it is the teachers who suffer the most abuse from government politicians when they campaign for better standards.

Truancy is a warning bell of family dysfunction and of parental indifference towards education. It is also a predictor of future trouble. A survey of adolescent girls in social welfare institutions showed that 95 percent of them had truanted, compared with 56 percent in the general community.

Lesley Max talked to Jim Taia, chief attendance officer of the now disbanded Auckland Education Board, who listed the following common aspects in the homes of truants: low socio-economic status; little understanding of the advantages of education; a short-term focus on life; both parents working, out of necessity, so that there is no one to see the children get off to school and no one to welcome them back at the end of the day; or 'poor solo mothers, having enough of a struggle just to exist, without worrying about truancy'. Taia referred to research showing that if children miss as few as seventeen days per year in their first two years of school, their education is in trouble. 'It's a waste of our time chasing up kids at high school. The effort ought to go in at primary level.'

The number of cases of truancy notified to the Children and Young Persons Service (CYPS) has jumped by 40 percent in the past year and is adding to the pressure on the cash-strapped agency, according to my colleague Annette King. In the latest budget, the service received only $11 million, when $25 million was the minimum required. The Minister of Social Welfare agreed with Labour's estimate of the amount of funding CYPS needed. He asked Cabinet for $60 million extra over three years but was rebuffed.

The underfunding means the Children and Young Persons Service does not have sufficient staff to do its job at a time when its workload is increasing. In West Auckland, schools have been asked to notify CYPS only of urgent cases of abuse. The manager of the Waitakere office sent a letter to West Auckland principals saying temporary staffing shortages meant his office could not cope with the volume of referrals.

As a recent *Press* editorial pointed out, many teachers these days face the prospect of instructing children who are toughened and rebellious before they even enter the classroom. 'Many, attuned to violent television, have a short attention span. Some exhibit this as a chronic condition, the so-called attention deficit disorder. The behaviour of others is not far from feral. That is an unhappy recipe for learning, disadvantaging not only those whose behaviour makes them almost impossible to teach, but also others who are keen to master what is on offer. Time given to establishing order is time lost from more productive activity.'

Formal school suspensions have nearly doubled since 1990. Government figures show that there were 7491 suspensions in 1994, up from 4207 in 1990. The steady rise in suspensions was a major concern to the Education and Science Select Committee during our Children at Risk Inquiry in 1994.

Some schools are going out of their way to help youngsters at risk, only to be clobbered by the bureaucrats. Papanui High School's Te Kaupapa Whakaroa programme is a creative initiative that is providing education, training and encouragement to at-risk youngsters. Most of them have gone through difficult times, most have been truants, and some have been in trouble with the law. But the school is struggling to get funding for the programme, because the bureaucrats can't decide whether money should come from education, health, police or income support budgets.

Each one of these children is in moral and physical danger. But each one is an opportunity. We know specifically where they live, we know who they are. We should target resources now. Nine thousand children disappear each year from our schools. Twenty thousand children play truant every day, and they are starting at a younger age. That's equivalent to the population of an entire city roaming our seats every school day. Where are the parents? There must be up to 40,000 truant mothers and fathers. Without action now, these children will be the villains of the future. The hard cases of today become the hardened criminals of tomorrow. When they reach prison, they will cost us $50,000 each per year.

Before the 1990 election, the National Party's education rhetoric included grand promises to lift the supposed tollgate on the road to knowledge, and to abolish tertiary fees. New Zealanders believed them, elected them, and were then aghast as the new National government cut millions of dollars from education spending, broke its promises to students and endangered the quality of public education. This has passed on an educational deficit to future generations, and will cost New Zealand dearly. The government's deficit has been abolished. The books balance. But students now have one and a half billion dollars in collective debt. Access to tertiary education is being rationed by the National government in the crudest manner possible.

David Caygill has pointed out that some physiotherapy students at the Auckland Institute of Technology are being charged fees of $11,000, while dental students at Otago University are paying $17,000. There is no reason why the government should decide how many physiotherapy students should be taught in Auckland, how many dental students should be taught in Dunedin, how many scientists at Canterbury or how many should study French or Russian at Victoria University. Those sorts of decisions can be perfectly and properly left to the institutions themselves. What the government is doing by limiting the number of places it will subsidise is simply limiting the opportunities available to New Zealand students.

For the third year running there has been a reported drop in first-year enrolments at tertiary institutions. This is a sign of a long-term problem in tertiary education. The main reason for the drop is that fees at tertiary institutions now average over $2400. Access to education under National has become more and more a matter of income. Middle-and low-income New Zealand families are unwilling to make a commitment to tertiary education because of the vast loans involved. Many students owe more than $30,000, a burden that can consign them to a lifetime of trying to service their debt.

Nearly 23,000 students received the unemployment benefit over the summer months because of the lack of summer employment opportunities. This problem occurs every year. These students are in financial strife because they are forced on to the unemployment benefit every summer. They are simply unable to earn and save enough money to cover the tuition fees and their ongoing living expenses. As soon as they enrol, students' unemployment benefit payments automatically cease because they are no longer eligible. Meanwhile they are unable to access the student allowance system because the staffing levels are totally inadequate to cope with the huge demands faced at the beginning of each academic year.

One student couple who returned to polytechnic were told they would have to wait four to six weeks before they could receive a student allowance. In the interim, they had nothing. They had to go cap-in-hand to banks to beg for credit to tide them over. I am told that a wait of more than four weeks is commonplace. It means that the students are left with no source of income at the time of year they need it most, for fees, new text books and accommodation.

One solution would be for the government to assist with job creation so that students could earn real money over the summer break. Earlier generations of hopeful students not only didn't have to face student fees, but could always find work during the Christmas holidays. The problem could also be eased if the staff who administer student allowances were part of the Income Support Service rather than part of each individual university or polytechnic. That way, there could be co-ordination so that the student allowance is started automatically when the unemployment benefit payments ended.

Many tertiary students who are forced to take out student loans to pay for their education may never own their own home. A young graduate couple brought to my attention had a combined debt of about $20,000. That is a considerably smaller debt than many students will find themselves starting their working lives with. Although they were both in secure employment, the bank wouldn't lend to them because they had an outstanding interest-bearing debt. They were told to come back when the student loan was paid off. Given that the minister's briefing papers indicate that 50 percent of students will still be paying back loans at the age of 40, and that more than 10 percent will still be paying at the age of 65, for thousands of young New Zealanders the prospect of ever owning their own home is bleak. Why don't we get these eager, talented young people to pay back their debts in time spent working for others in the community during the holidays, gaining work experience, receiving a modest income and paying back their student debts? Labour's policy of a dollar-for-dollar subsidy on early repayment of debt provides an added incentive.

New technologies offer opportunities as well as potential barriers for the children of the poor. Information networks such as the Internet have the potential to liberate the poor by giving them the same access to information as their better-off counterparts. But there are already clear signs that the new technology is more likely to accelerate the gap between rich and poor, creating a two-tiered society of information 'haves' and 'have-nots'. The cost of the computers and software necessary to access the Internet is way beyond the pockets of most poor families in New Zealand.

Research in the United States suggests that traditional blue-collar workers and their families are becoming increasingly marginalised as information 'have-nots'. By the end of 1995 it was estimated that 40 million Americans were using networked information services from home. Only 12.7 percent of them were living in households earning less than US$15,000. Proportional use of other media technologies such as telephones, radios, videos and television was far more balanced across income levels than the individual use of networked information.

American statistics also highlight significant ethnic variations in computer ownership. Just under 30 percent of white households have computers, compared to 13.4 percent of black households, 12.6 percent of native American households and 12.4 percent of Hispanic households.

There have been calls in the United States for policies that encourage a levelling effect between information haves and have-nots. A universal service policy has been suggested that would combine market incentives and individual tax credits to increase computer ownership among low-income households, promote development of public-access network services, and fund network literacy programmes through schools, public libraries and adult education programmes. We need to consider similar initiatives in this country, to help break the cycle and minimise the development of an 'information poor'.

New Zealand pioneered distance education through the radio. Our grandparents built public libraries as the first social call on ratepayers. We now lack the wit and the vision to see the future. Nations and individuals will be rich or poor, successes or failures depending on their ability to access the new technology. Every school should be on the Internet.

The success of kohanga reo and the Pacific Island language nests is proof that community involvement can and does work, but overall educational achievement among Maori remains a serious concern. Although Maori achievement has improved in recent years, it has not kept pace with improvements in the general population.

A staggering 35.8 percent of Maori who left school last year had gained no formal qualification. Pacific Island students fared a little better, although 24.3 percent left with no qualification. The overall figure for school leavers was 18.1 percent. Maori spend on average 4.1 years at secondary school, compared with 4.4 percent for Pacific Island children and 4.6 percent for Pakeha children. Only 4 percent of Maori and 5.6 percent of Pacific Island students left school in 1995 with a pass in Bursary. This compares with an overall rate of 19 percent. In tertiary education, Maori are most likely to enrolled in polytechnics, while non-Maori are most likely to be enrolled in universities. Where Maori are enrolled at university, they are likely to be attending only part time. There are more Asians and overseas students than Maori at some New Zealand universities.

When I look into the faces of sixth and seventh formers, I see young adults who ask only for the same kind of chances Jim Bolger and I had – but ignored – when we were young. Why should this generation have to accept that they are not going to have the same start in life that their parents had?

We need to take a wider approach to education. In places like South Auckland, where glue ear is prevalent among children, the issues of health and education are interrelated. Children will be more successful at school if they are healthy; if there is nourishing food in their stomachs. Eliminating the health problems will have a positive spin-off on education of our young.

More home-based support must be provided for parents and young children. The budget for early childhood education session subsidies needs to be significantly increased so that group sizes can be reduced. Extra money is also needed to accommodate growing early childhood education rolls, and to tackle maintenance and building needs. Children in poor communities and rural areas are often unable to take advantage of early childhood education. An equity funding system is needed to help compensate for the lack of resources available to low-income communities. Barriers to setting up kohanga reo and Pacific Island language groups must be removed. The Correspondence School's early-childhood programme should receive extra funding, as should mobile kindergartens.

Funds cut from school operating grants since 1990 should be restored, and adjusted every year to keep abreast of costs. Equity funding should be doubled for schools in poorer areas. The right of every child to attend their local school should be guaranteed. Bulk funding of teachers' salaries should be scrapped, as should the voucher scheme for private schools. New schools need to be built to meet population needs, and we need to immediately tackle the repairs needed to bring existing buildings up to standard.

Class sizes must be reduced, particularly in junior classes and poorer schools. A central database should be set up to ensure students no longer drop out of the system. More funding is needed for teaching English to children for whom it is not the first language, so that the education of these students and their classmates is not held back. We should properly recognise the importance of early childhood education by supporting pay parity between primary and secondary teachers. Teachers need to be properly rewarded for the crucial roles they play in the economy, and funds should also be provided to train teachers and counsellors to help children at risk and reduce truancy and disruptive behaviour in class.

Nobody in New Zealand should be denied access to tertiary education because they can't afford it. Student allowances should be increased to the level of the unemployment benefit, and should be given to sixteen- and seventeen-year-olds in full-time study. Access to allowances should be widened, and the means test on parental income should be progressively abolished. Students should have access to the same accommodation supplement available to other low-income people. Student fees should be lowered to $1000 per year for all full-time courses, so that young people can choose the course that suits their interests and abilities, rather than their pockets. We should raise the income threshold before repayment of students loans is required, from the present $14,300 to $25,000 a year. Interest should not be charged while students are still studying. We should make it easier for former students to clear their debts by matching dollar for dollar any payment above the minimum required. So if a former student is required to pay $500, but pays $400 more, the government should match this and write off $400 of their debt. This should apply to up to 50 percent of their actual course costs and fees.

Funding needs to be increased for Maori initiatives at all educational levels, including kohanga reo, kura kaupapa and wananga. More money should also be invested to increase the number of Maori teachers and teachers competent in te reo and nga tikanga Maori.

We want our children to grow into good citizens and taxpayers of the future. They deserve their share of the New Zealand dream. We cannot afford to waste a single person. The welfare state was created to provide fairness and social justice. We can't run our small country on the skills of the 10 percent of children whose parents have the deepest pockets. We need to encourage our future leaders from all classes, areas, races and genders.

Everything we do in the name of developing the nation, making it economically strong, a decent place to live and grow old in, we do in the name of New Zealand's children. The challenge to us all is not to betray the faith and the hope our young people have in us. They expect, as we expected of our parents, to inherit a society and a country in which they can take pride and do better. They simply ask for the same opportunities to learn skills to prepare them for a demanding future. Giving them an education that will allow them to take on the world is probably the most precious gift they will ever receive.

four

The Victims of Violence

YOUNG NEW ZEALANDERS today are more likely to be the victims of violence – or more likely to commit violent acts – than at any other time in our nation's short history. The shocking details of a recent series of child deaths have stunned the nation. Tens of thousands of cases of child abuse or neglect are notified in New Zealand each year, and many more go unreported.

Lawyer Simon Jefferson told Lesley Max that the extent of child abuse and child neglect is far greater than New Zealand society accepts or is willing to accept it to be. 'The formal response to the problem is feeble, at a legal level, at an intervention level, and at a prevention level.' In a speech to primary teachers in 1995, Commissioner for Children Laurie O'Reilly said children endure mental abuse, sibling abuse, are exploited sexually, witness spouse abuse, and seven had been murdered by their care-givers in the previous twelve months. Many of the complaints to the Children's Commissioner are school-related. O'Reilly has spoken of a 'conspiracy of silence, processes of intimidation, and pressure on whistleblowers. What I can't understand is how informed parents [and] caring teachers could be part of that? How have we developed a tolerance to violence?'

Lesley Max argues that New Zealanders of Pakeha, Maori and Pacific Island backgrounds are 'culturally wedded' to the practice of hitting children. She points to studies showing that even well-educated prosperous Pakeha parents hit their children, a practice that, in American terms, might be identifed as borderline abuse. A quote from a recent *Wanganui Chronicle* article on child abuse provided a graphic illustration: 'Mark's mum is pregnant. When his dad is angry, he tells Mark to kick his mum in the tummy. After he's done it, his dad praises him. Mark has learnt that violence earns him rewards. Now he's kicking his two-year-old sister. No local pre-school will have him.'

Eleven-year-old Craig Manukau was dragged from a school disco by his drunken father and kicked to death. The mother and stepfather of two-year-old Delcelia Witika repeatedly beat and scalded her, then left her to die while they went to a party. Three-year-old Jordan Asby died after his stepfather punched him and hit him with a belt. Eleven-year-old Wayne-Marshall Kairau was murdered by his stepfather, who then burned his body in a 44-gallon drum. Twelve-year-old Dane Gibson was bludgeoned to death with a concrete paving stone by parents, who thought he was possessed by the devil.

Former Commissioner for Children Ian Hassell told *North and South* magazine in 1994 that a number of deaths attributed to accidents 'were very likely homicide'. He estimated that the rate at which children were killed was double the official rate.

Laurie O'Reilly says government attempts to protect children from violence, sexual abuse and discrimination are not working. 'Services are not available, we lack resources, there are gaps between policy and practice, inadequate guidelines, lack of support for staff, lack of information, and a not-my-responsibility syndrome.' The commissioner believes that laws enacted to keep families together and protect privacy are often making things worse: 'The very legislation designed to protect those vulnerable children has been used as a sword against them.'

Delegates at the Investing in Children conference in Dunedin in July 1996 expressed widespread concern about the implementation of the Children, Young Persons and their Families Act. Family lawyer June Johnston talked of a 'crisis of catastrophic proportions'. The head of Otago University's Children's Issues Centre, Professor Anne Smith, said that although the Act was thought to be 'an enlightened piece of good legislation', many thought it was not being applied properly or resourced adequately. Problems included a lack of good preventative social work, high turnover of social work staff, low staff morale, continual restructuring, inability to follow children who move, problems with family group conferences, slowness to act on complaints, and inadequate care and protection of children. The conference recommended that an independent official inquiry be set up to investigate the implementation of the Act, and the role of the Children, Young Persons and their Families Service.

There is a crisis in the service. Social workers in Christchurch have told me that children's lives are at risk because of a lack of resources. This is not an exaggeration. My colleague Annette King points out that social workers are unable to cope with overwhelming workloads, and morale is non-existent. Social workers are voting with their feet and walking out. New Zealand has lost 252 social workers in less than 24 months. This represents a loss of more than 1200 years' collective experience. To make up for the shortfall, the government has employed only 149 new, inexperienced social workers. Children are not getting the care and consideration they deserve.

According to the government's own figures, more than 800 reports of child abuse in Auckland went uninvestigated in an eight-month period between July 1995 and February 1996. Dunedin Care and Protection Panel chairwoman Kathryn Lucas told the *Otago Daily Times* that people had stopped reporting their suspicions of child abuse to the CYPFS for fear that nothing would be done because of the lack of resources. Overspending in the service's Dunedin office meant that restrictions were being placed on dealing with all but the most extreme referrals of abuse.

In a paper released to Labour under the Official Information Act, the Minister of Social Welfare conceded that increases in juvenile offending, home-alone cases, expulsions from schools, and reports of violence against women and children had increased the service's workload. Gresham sought an extra $60 million funding over three years, but was only able to convince Treasury and his colleagues to provide half that amount. The government has poured money into funding television advertising encouraging children and parents to report abuse, which has stimulated a huge additional burden on top of the existing workload. Abused children need specialist counselling and professional care and protection. It is outrageous that youngsters who have been assessed as needing care have to wait an average of 97 days for a bed in a protection centre or youth justice unit.

The director of Hamilton's Parentline counselling service, Maxine Hodgson, has expressed concern about the growing number of calls about child abuse from families living in rural communities. She told the *New Zealand Herald* that more people are seeking a rural lifestyle, but are not part of the rural community: 'Access to social services in rural areas is only obvious if one is part of the community on a social interaction basis.' She warned that some rural cottages available at cheap rental were not suitable for children.

Sally Jackman's research shows that rates of reported child abuse tend to be higher in poorer areas. She notes, however, that these same communities tend to be subject to higher levels of surveillance, and therefore 'reporting' might be at a higher rate than less observed areas. 'The argument that poverty caused child abuse appears to focus around the notion that poverty causes stress and that stress leads to child abuse. Other approaches focus on a more complex systems approach, whereby a web of problems are seen to cause abuse, including notions of social disintegration. The abusing family or parent may be isolated socially, without a strong and supportive community.' Jackman concludes that whatever the approach, it is clear that poverty is part of the child-abuse problem, and that poverty puts enormous pressures on families.

It is clear that criminal offending by young people is increasing. Last year over 43,000 young offenders were apprehended, an increase of 39 percent since National took office. The number of juveniles apprehended by the police for violent offences jumped from 1839 in 1990 to 4058 in 1995. More than 90 children aged under ten were apprehended for violence in 1995, compared with just 37 five years earlier. More than 800 children aged from ten to thirteen, and 3100 youngsters aged between fourteen and sixteen were apprehended for violence in 1995. For both age groups these figures were well over double the rates in 1990.

Since the introduction of the Children, Young Persons and their Families Act, most cases involving young people have been dealt with outside formal prosecution processes in court. Statistics from the Wanganui computer are collected on a regular basis only for cases that are prosecuted in court, so information on the majority of cases involving youth offenders is not available. Many young offenders are dealt with at family group conferences, or by some other means such as a warning from the police, without an appearance in court.

Of the 3886 cases that did go to court in 1995, just over a quarter involved a violent offence. Ministry of Justice figures show that the number of prosecutions for violent sexual offences involving young people rose from 21 in 1991 to 37 in 1995. The number of aggravated robbery prosecutions jumped from 46 to 117 over the same period, and serious assaults involving young people rose from 41 to 90.

The offenders are getting younger and the crimes more serious. Some youths are treating life as 'one big party', according to the head of Dunedin's crime squad, Detective Senior Sergeant Peter Gibbons. He told the *Otago Daily Times* that juveniles have no qualms about committing crime to maintain their lifestyle: 'Your older offender might commit one burglary every couple of months. These juveniles go on crime sprees. They could easily do five burglaries in a day.' The police were aware of several houses in Dunedin in which large numbers of teenagers lived. 'They're the sort of places where you get four people sleeping in a bedroom. They are generally juveniles away from home and have no parental control. Their only income is the independent youth benefit. Their lifestyle exceeds the benefit, so they commit crimes.'

Juvenile offenders are themselves becoming the victims of the government's failure to provide enough room in Social Welfare institutions. Judges are being forced to place youths in police cells or return them to the community because of a shortage of secure placements. In July 1996 a sixteen-year-old youth was forced to spend thirteen nights in a Christchurch police cell because there was nowhere else for him to be sent. Laurie O'Reilly warned that young people in police cells were exposed to a parade of adult criminals, who were often drunk, violent and abusive.

Christchurch police youth aid spokesperson, Sergeant Chris Roper, told *The Press* that the lack of custodial facilities for repeat young offenders was having a flow-on effect on the crime rate: 'We are talking about young people aged sixteen having more than 40 criminal convictions. These are not kids stealing chocolate fish from Deka. They are committing serious crime.'

In August 1996 the *Sunday Star-Times* revealed that the Family Court had been placing young offenders in the care of the leader of Wairarapa's notorious Nomads gang; a man who at the time of writing was serving a jail sentence for drug offences, extortion, threatening and assault. This was done with official support from the authorities, who knew the man's background. Does this mean that we now pay for the gangs to recruit young people?

Gangs that used to live off burglaries and theft to order are now operating what are effectively drug supermarkets. Police estimate that 80 percent of the illegal drugs in New Zealand are retailed by, or for, gang members. Their customers include children in school uniforms.

Forty percent of non-domestic homicides in the last three years have been gang related. The gangs inhabit a place known as the underworld – a world most Kiwis know nothing about. It is called the underworld because it is. They are called outlaws not only because they live outside the law, but also outside the laws of normal civilised behaviour expected of the rest of us.

Racial hatred is used as powerful recruitment and management tools for evil and ruthless gang leaders. They hold gangs together, and are yet another timebomb ticking away.

Most other western societies are wrestling with similar problems. The alienation, hatred and unemployment on which gangs feed are not unique to New Zealand. In the United States, the vulnerable communities of African Americans, Asian Americans and Hispanics are being drawn into extended gang families. Two generations ago it was the immigrant Italian community. In France, Holland and Germany, Algerian, North African and Turkish youths have organised themselves into gangs for mutual affection and protection. They are responding to the social evils of racism, unemployment and, according to criminologists, the most powerful of all destructive factors – hopelessness.

Young people are the victims of this age of cynicism, despair, pessimism and physical fear. Too many of our school children don't believe they will ever have a job, a family or a home in the conventional sense. They face middle-aged burnout at seventeen.

Families are breaking down, and our societies are experiencing the whirlwind of third generation unemployment and drug-taking.

Maori, Pacific Island and Pakeha youth took to the streets in Christchurch in July 1996 to protest at the growing racial and street violence in the city. The march followed the death of a sixteen-year-old who was stabbed several times in the chest during a brawl. A friend of the young victim told *The Press* that racism was a serious ongoing problem in the city, fuelled by tensions between Polynesians and skinheads. 'Kids should be able to go out and enjoy themselves. Instead, we are constantly worried about our safety and have to watch our backs. We don't want to be prisoners in our own homes.'

It is a sad fact that many gangs are dominated by young Maori. They are the most vulnerable. Maori continue to be grossly over-represented in crime statistics. On average, 155 out of every 1000 Maori were apprehended by the police for a crime in 1995. The corresponding figure for non-Maori was 39 out of every 1000.

The movie *Once Were Warriors* was more like a documentary than an adaptation of a novel. Maori gangs are operating on a mutant cultural basis. The romantic view of the warrior has been perverted. Black Power gang leaders even have the gall to claim that they are the victims of racism. It is the public and the vulnerable children drawn into their evil webs who are the victims. The Treaty of Waitangi has got nothing to do with selling drugs, prostitution, protection rackets and counterfeiting. It is an insult to Maoridom for these gangsters to pose as victims. Claims of racism by Black Power are as outrageous as claims by members of the white Road Knights gang that they are genetically superior.

Some New Zealand gangs have evolved into sophisticated crime organisations. They are a different breed to the 'hoons' of the 1970s. Their leaders drive limousines, they run escort businesses, and deal in large quantities of illegal drugs. Some gangs hire conservative lawyers who help shield their criminal activities behind seemingly respectable businesses. Angry police officers tell me they have seen a Black Power photograph of an estimated quarter of a million dollars on a table. Others have told me that gang members pay for new houses with cash. The

Police Commissioner warns that New Zealand has just five years to deal with this form of organised crime, before it becomes too big to control.

We have been given a wake-up call. New Zealand's age of innocence is over. Many New Zealanders have been surprised and shocked to learn through the news media of the growing links between our gangs and international crime syndicates. Sadly, the media are only reporting the tip of the iceberg.

Asian triads operate in our prisons. They employ New Zealand gang members to give them protection. These are the people who have put contracts out on New Zealand police officers. Gangs provide the muscle and disciplined 'soldiers' to carry out the distribution of drugs, and run the prostitution and protection rackets. A leaked police report has revealed the plans of the international Banditos motorcycle gang to muscle in on New Zealand's illegal drug industry. A New Zealander has recently served as world secretary for the Hell's Angels organisation. Three Hell's Angels members in Auckland wear 'Filthy Few' badges, an 'honour' they receive if they murder someone. These people travel regularly overseas. Why? Police believe they could be contract killers. They know they are being watched.

July 12, 1996 was a day of shame for New Zealand. An undercover policeman was forced to fly out of the country of his birth, leaving behind a sick mother, because of threats made by gangs to him and his family. Undercover police officers are heroes. They risk their lives, their health and their families to protect us from gangs and organised criminals who terrorise us and sell drugs to our children. It is shameful that we are not prepared to, at the very least, give undercover police the same assistance we give to informers through the witness-protection scheme.

Relocating people through the witness protection scheme is a legitimate and important part of modern policing. But here we had the situation where an informer was relocated, but the officer who recruited the informer was left dangerously vulnerable. I'm told there are more than 30 officers seeking help from the police because of problems of drug addiction as a result of their work. Most have seen their marriages, as well as their health, collapse. They deserve all the help we can give them.

We are blessed in New Zealand with an honest police force and judiciary, but we must act decisively to keep it that way. The challenge is to prevent New Zealand becoming like New South Wales, where corruption of the police, judges and politicians is commonplace.

The gangs are clearly more organised than the government. The gang member who pulls the trigger in a drive-by shooting and injures an innocent bystander is entitled to counselling once he is convicted and goes to prison. But the ten-year-old boy in the back seat of the car who witnesses his mother being shot is refused counselling and assistance from the Accident Compensation Corporation. It is morally indefensible that this could happen in New Zealand, but it did – in Christchurch in 1996.

Roger Douglas has suggested that the root cause of crime lies in the social welfare system itself, because it takes away a person's responsibilties for their decisions and robs them of the ability to stand on their own two feet. He argues that the billions of dollars New Zealand spends on social welfare is part of the problem, not the solution: 'Our current welfare system rewards family disintegration and dependency on the state rather than encouraging personal responsibility and independence. It encourages the growth of single parent families. The welfare system even promises you income and a house as long as you don't work or marry someone who does work. This perpetuates dysfunctional families, increasing lack of personal responsiblity and loss of dignity, all of which often lead to crime.' Sir Roger's solution is to scrap the domestic purposes benefit. That's a cheap shot and won't work.

ACT produces some of the best research about the problems, but also produces the worst policies, drawn from misguided and extreme conclusions. ACT is like the old Marxists who claimed that capitalism was the problem. Abolish capitalism, they said, and you would abolish theft and crime. Roger Douglas has pointed out that a child born into a family where there is existing criminal behaviour, violence, drug use, alcoholism and sexual abuse is 100 times more likely to seriously offend against society than a child born into a normal, caring family. These dysfunctional families are responsible for 80 percent of serious crime in New Zealand. 'We know these things,' he says, 'yet current policies (such as the domestic purposes benefit) encourage children born into these families to have children of their own at a very early age. Why in these circumstances do we continue to support a welfare system that creates the very behaviour that it is supposedly intended to stop?'

The Right blames do-gooders. Winston Peters also attacks them, calling them sickly white liberals. I'm proud to be a sickly white liberal. It is the do-gooders who run Meals on Wheels, Citizens Advice Bureaux, food kitchens, rugby clubs and the Salvation Army. The sickly white liberals freed the slaves, fought to give women the vote and abolished child labour. And what's wrong with being a do-gooder? We can never have enough of them.

Why do so many of our young people turn to violence? Victoria University criminologist John Pratt points to a national insecurity complex. He told the *Dominion* in 1994 that the ideal Kiwi is still the strong, silent rugby type. 'It's not very easy for men to communicate with others if they have problems which need solving,' he said. 'Violence has become a too-ready solution. Going right back to the days of colonisation, New Zealand has always had a sense of insecurity because it has been very cut off, has a small population, and has had to deal with an indigenous population. Once you remove the levels of control that governments used to impose, it only adds to the sense of insecurity.' Pratt also argued that New Zealand culture was reflected in an obsession with crime by the main television news programmes, which perpetuated a climate of fear of crime: 'The whole pitch and tone of the news is always about anxieties and troubles, much more so than in Britain.'

Our children are being exposed to television violence from very early ages. Even programmes targeted at preschoolers often contain graphic scenes of violence. Lesley Max complains of an 'insidious revolution in public entertainment, which has created a "cultural" climate for young people of violence, perverted sexuality and horror unprecedented in modern history. It has given rise to whole new genres of entertainment, such as "splatter movies" and "bad taste" movies. It has seen family homes become what seedy clubs used to be, a place for watching pornography – only then it was furtive and now it is "family style".'

She says there is no public concern about the fear that children suffer from exposure to material that is 'designed, with all the ingenuity money can buy, to terrify'. In August 1996, children were watching movies with titles like *A Time to Kill* and *Primal Fear.* Even advertisements for the matinée sessions of *Flipper* warned that the movie contained violence.

The need to protect children from abuse and neglect can no longer be ignored. There is an urgent need to improve the responsiveness of crisis-intervention services for families. There are many skilled and dedicated people in community-based agencies and Social Welfare services who work hard to meet the needs of children and families in crisis. Sadly, their efforts are being undermined by a lack of adequate resources. The National government has allowed funding in this area to fall well behind the increases in the volume of need. Although the budget is in surplus, National continues to sacrifice the well-being of children by refusing to resource care and protection services adequately.

Funding for the Children and Young Persons Service must be increased immediately, both to recognise the increased workload and to provide for improved training of staff. And funding must be maintained at a level sufficient to enable staff to investigate cases promptly.

In July 1996 – three months out from the general election – the government announced new laws on gangs after saying for three years that there was no need for new laws or resources. Despite the cynical timing of the measures, the government deserved two cheers for taking some first, albeit tentative, steps. The moves ignored, however, the need for zero tolerance of gangs. We need a New Zealand-wide strategy to beat the gangs, before it is too late. It is pointless continuing with the policing tactics of the 1960s and 70s, because the size and shape of the problem has changed dramatically.

We need a national crime authority that brings together the police, Inland Revenue Department, Customs, Department of Corrections, Labour Department, Immigration Service, Ministry of Foreign Affairs and Trade, and even the Security Intelligence Service. Every time a gang member travels overseas, opens a business, imports or exports a product, applies for a benefit, joins a work scheme or goes to prison, a light should sparkle on a police computer. The parliamentary select committee that studied gangs eventually supported my idea for a national crime authority, which was flattering considering the committee had a majority of National members and given that National ministers opposed the concept.

Gang members prefer to go to prison rather than endure the humiliation of periodic detention and physical work. They need the comradeship of fellow gang members. Our punishment regimes reinforce gang discipline and control. We need a new type of imprisonment that involves manual work. One option would be to follow an approach being considered by the US Senate and say that any crime committed by a gang member will attract an automatic doubling of the penalty, whether it be for a traffic offence or rape. That would help break up the gangs. They wouldn't hang around the courts, showing off and intimidating people. Their lawyers would be trying to argue that their clients were not gang members, an argument that would strike at the heart of gang recruitment.

Civil libertarians and gang leaders will oppose this. There are those who say you cannot single out gangs for special attention, but Parliament has already voted to introduce legislation which does exactly that. New non-association laws will mean that gang members who commit crimes can be instructed by the courts not to associate with other gang members. So the principle of special treatment for gang members has already been accepted by Parliament.

Gang members should be treated more harshly than others because they operate a pyramid management system. Recruitment and promotion of young propects is based on how many crimes they commit. Some gangs have rules that you must go to jail, must participate in gang rape and commit odious and evil deeds to get your promotion 'patch'. We must make gang membership so unattractive that vulnerable young people will not be enticed into this sordid, corrupt world.

Gang fortifications should be demolished, but knocking them down is only part of the answer. Gangs will simply retreat to industrial areas, or buy ten-acre blocks and continue their criminal work. Out of sight is not out of mind. Gangs should not be reinforced by taxpayer-subsidised work schemes. It is unacceptable that the government keeps no records of the number of gang members on work schemes. We should have the guts to get rid of schemes and projects that fail. No taxpayer money should be handed out to gang members. Parents can also be held more responsible. Perhaps some parents ought to do periodic detention with their children.

Criminals are generally not born; they are made and they are made early in their lives. We need policies which ensure that all children get a decent start in life rather than begin with attitudes distorted by abuse, neglect and poor role modelling. Inter-generational cycles of abuse, neglect and poverty can be broken by effective early intervention. Schools need to be given more help to deal earlier and effectively with disruptive and violent behaviour by children. Positive recreational activities are needed for children from at-risk and disadvantaged families. Communities are entitled to protection from serious and recidivist offending by a small hard core of violent juvenile offenders who need to be kept in secure custody while being worked with to change their behaviour. We need to adequately resource community-based prevention and rehabilitation programmes with proven records of success. Programmes are needed to encourage prisoners to change their attitude, to develop work skills, work habits and work experience, and to address the cause of their criminal behaviour, such as alcohol and drug addiction and mental disorder. A tougher stance should be taken against recidivist criminals who reject rehabilitation opportunities, through longer sentences, less parole and zero tolerance of offences committed on leave.

There must also be alternatives apart from returning youths to the environment, family or peer group that led to their offending in the first place. We should create a new programme with professionally trained foster parents and mentors to which difficult young people can be referred. Young offenders should be encouraged to join the armed services, where they will gain discipline, self-esteem and can learn a trade. Unless we act now to deal with this problem, and the underlying factors leading to a growth in juvenile crime, today's juvenile offenders will become tomorrow's adult career criminals.

Labour pioneered recognition of victims' rights in the Victims of Offences Act 1987. It is now time to build on that record to ensure that the justice system is legally accountable for the way it treats victims of crime. I wrote a victims' charter for the 1993 election. You have seen on television how the police read out the rights of a criminal when being arrested – but you have never seen a victim have his or her rights read out.

Civilised society functions on public social censorship; on a clear understanding and acceptance of what is right and wrong. Gangs operate on an extended family system based on perverted values. It's okay to steal or smoke dope. You're a hero if you rape someone and go to prison. You get promoted within the gang structure. Group approval is based on the amount of havoc you create. Values systems have been turned upside down, and children are the innocent victims.

As Lesley Max says, 'A society that can care about the Southland beech forest, the kokako and Muroroa Atoll – a society that professes to be struggling for equity and justice for all – must care about its most vulnerable members, its smallest members, its wordless members, and about those who have the power of life and death, joy and misery, over them.'

There is enough blame for all politicians and parties to share over our collective failure to deal with gangs in New Zealand. The idea that we could get gang members into constructive work and wean them away from their criminal activities was a good idea that failed. We ought to admit it. At the risk of infuriating the social apologists and the politically correct, let's accept that the churches and volunteer groups have had more success to date than most departmental schemes at getting people to leave gangs.

But let's not condone the recent suggestions by some church leaders that crime is understandable, even acceptable, if people are poor. This is wrong, dangerous and a sellout. It is no help to offer no hope to the young. And let's not hide behind cultural safety, or confuse the young with mixed messages of liberal acceptance of cannabis, while banning advertising of cigarettes.

The word 'punishment' has become unfashionable and politically incorrect. We must not mediate or argue for a truce or peace with gangs. That would play right into their hands. They want the problem out of the headlines, so they can continue their criminal work. Future generations of New Zealanders will curse us if we fail to recognise the dangerous role that racial hatred plays in the day to day lives of gangs. The silence of Maori and church leaders on this point has been disappointing. Perhaps they have become too intimidated by the politically correct. They are not the Easy Riders of the 60s. Civil libertarians have asked, why single out the gangs? What about the Salvation Army, Rotary? When we have evidence these organisations are involved in gang rape, extortion, drug-dealing, intimidation of witnesses, and so on, we should move against them. But as yet there is no evidence to link them to organised crime.

United States experts have been warning for some time of a tidal wave of extreme youth violence. Ten-year-olds have raped, murdered and sold drugs. They are cruelly manipulated by the more seasoned villains, who know that the youngsters will escape the criminal courts because they are not treated as adults. Gangs in New Zealand use these children to escape our legal process. They are called 'prospects'. By later passing certain tests, they graduate into full-blown 'patch' members.

Inspector Chris Graveson, the head of youth aid at Police National Headquarters, told the *Sunday Star-Times* in September 1996 that New Zealand was already 'gripped in a teenage crime wave which, if not halted, would become chronic as the young population grows over the next decade'. He noted that 45 percent of all robberies are now committed by children aged under seventeen, and said, 'It doesn't take a genius to work out what's going to happen as the population for those age groups increases.'

If we fail to come up with solutions to youth and organised crime in New Zealand, our country will become like the no-go areas of Los Angeles. Then the real criminals will be us.

five

The Death of Common Sense

IF YOU are aged over sixty, PC probably means police constable. If you are under twenty, it probably means personal computer. If you are a republican New Zealand prime minister, PC probably means Privy Councillor, a title proudly awarded to yourself, representing membership of the Queen's advisory council, which you have sworn to abolish. But to the majority of people, PC now means politically correct.

Parents are being bombarded by extremists and control freaks who have captured the English language. This modern manifestation of political correctness has coincided with – and accelerated – the demise of the family unit. The concepts of family and values that have stood strong and consistent for generations are under siege, and the ultimate victims are the children, who are on the receiving end of a confusing array of mixed messages.

Choice, and even the arrangement, of words can change perceptions. For example, eating a lamb's leg sounds awful, but eating a leg of lamb sounds acceptable. Language also evolves. The family joint on a Sunday has an additional meaning for the children of today, as do the words 'grass' and 'gay'. The guardians of political correctness would argue that I am no longer bald, but follically challenged. Ruth Richardson can seek a political comeback because she's no longer short; she's vertically challenged. No one is opposed to sensitivity. But things have gone too far, crossing into the realm of self-imposed censorship by those who have been intimidated into silence.

Political correctness is not new. It is an old totalitarian concept. It asserts the right of those in positions of power to suppress all but their own party lines, official lies and positions. When churches had power, those who opposed the official line were heretics or witches, to be burnt at the stake. In the days of the monarchy, it was high treason to suggest the king had no clothes. Indeed, there is still a law on the British books to make it a capital offence to bed a royal outside marriage. The hangman would be a busy person if the law was implemented in modern-day England. Communications provided a new form of political power that was perfected by the Nazis and Stalinists in the 1930s. Their techniques were similar to those of today: intimidation, character assassination and denial of free speech and thought.

The first blitzkrieg was an intellectual one, targeted at the control of university curricula and the intimidation of the news media. It was successful. In 1927 French writer Julius Benda published a bestseller, *The Treason of the Intellectuals*, which exposed scholars and writers for their cowardice, lust for power and their opportunism. He claimed that, by suspending their critical and objective powers of reasoning, they abrogated their responsibility, ignored their intellectual duty, betrayed their values and joined the barbarians of the Right and Left.

These days even the Bible is no longer sacred. It is being re-written and de-sexed. The politically correct Bible now says Jesus didn't sit on the right hand of God, because this discriminates against left-handed people. Venus de Milo is probably okay because she now has no arms, but the politically correct have yet to look at Michelangelo's David, who discriminates against the circumcised.

The Good Samaritan story may yet be rewritten thus: A person was beaten and robbed on the road to Jericho. The priests saw the distraught man but walked on, as did the politicians. However, a social worker spied the bleeding and beaten man, rushed up to him and cried, 'Good Lord! Whoever did this to you needs help.'

Hans Christian Anderson, the Brothers Grimm, even Aesop is no longer safe. Snow White will take refuge with seven vertically challenged men. Poor Little Red Riding Hood will encounter a cross-dressing wolf, and the Three Little Pigs will build environmentally safe homes out of indigenous products. Noddy books have been rewritten. One of the more absurd manifestations of 'correctness' was the argument that Greenlane Hospital should destroy a mural in the children's ward which pictured Pinocchio, because it supposedly manipulated children. The Auckland City Council will pay for a Christmas festival, but not carols by candlelight, because it is religious. Last Easter, a Wellington kindergarten banned hot cross buns because the crosses might have offended non-Christians. We should allow and celebrate all religions and cultures, where they are represented.

Children need to know what is good and what is bad. Extreme liberals keep telling parents and the public that we need a values-neutral education system. What does that mean? A teacher refused to take a class to *Romeo and Juliet* because it 'promoted heterosexuality'. Another corrected 'manhole' to 'personhole' in a New Plymouth child's essay. (The teacher was actually out of date: according to one PC handbook, the word is now 'femhole'.) The *Dictionary of Gender-Free Usage* suggests the term 'utility access hole'.

The morality and ethics of the so-called neutral-value concept in education have not been fully debated. Parents must rule. They must have the power, not new-age educationalists.

The bureaucratically correct reached new heights of confusion when the Education Ministry's early childhood manager was reported as saying that the ministry did not fund childcare providers, but bought the services they provided. I recently heard of an incident involving a six-year-old American child who was 'caught' kissing a female student. It was a peck on the cheek in front of the class and teacher. The boy's parents were given a note and a lecture about sexual abuse. The little boy was interviewed on television. He didn't know what the adults were talking about. He simply said the girl was his friend. The incident was harmless, and the parents of both children were outraged.

I wonder how many kisses, full frontals, shootings, murders and acts of sexual violence a child sees on television before he or she is six? We ought to have the toughest anti-violence stance in the world, not the softest. Yet we have many programmes on our free-to-air television during family hours that are only available on cable in America.

The furore over the Maori girl who featured in a Telecom advertisement was particularly misdirected. Young Jamie was accused of failing to speak Maori, and criticised for not being surrounded by her whanau and for singing an English song rather than a Maori waiata. This criticism came from a former governor-general. The girl and her parents were infuriated. Her father pointed out that she spoke Maori and had appeared in several New Zealand dramas promoting Maoridom. The parents were proud of her obvious talents. It was insulting to call her a token figure.

We no longer have hospitals. We have CHEs, or Crown Health Enterprises. In South Australia, no one dies in a hospital, but they do have negative patient outcomes. You are still dead, but I guess it looks better on a balance sheet. A Wellington hospital solemnly insisted that psychiatric patients sign a legal form promising not to commit suicide. A blood-stained copy was found on one young ex-patient who took his own life. Parents, taxpayers and students have a right to ask, 'What the hell is going on?'

The law is being contorted to provide excuses for anti-social behaviour. The old joke about the boy who, after murdering his parents, sought mercy from the courts because he was an orphan, is no longer just a joke. 'Adopted child syndrome' was used as a defence by Joel Rifkin, who murdered seventeen prostitutes on Long Island. 'Foetal trimethadione syndrome' – sadism resulting from a mother's epilepsy medication during pregnancy – was blamed in court for a teenager's brutal murder of a four-year-old.

The family in all its shapes has been the basic unit in every society, every civilisation, every great religion throughout the ages. Why? Because it works, because it is right. Therefore policies and programmes that support families are good. Those that split families or encourage the destruction of families are bad. The assault on family values by the politically correct has coincided with growing economic pressures. Children are the innocents caught in the crossfire of this double-barrelled bombardment.

The United Nations Children's Fund has identified the root causes of child neglect in so-called rich nations as new forms of scarcity in both public resources and parental time: 'In the

Anglo-American world, this failure to invest in children has been aggravated by a growing time deficit. Over the last two decades, there has been a sharp decline in the amount of time parents spend caring for their children.'

The trend is seen as particularly pronounced in the United Kingdom and United States, but the symptoms, as explained by Stanford University economist Victor Fuchs, will be familiar to many New Zealand parents: 'The time parents have available for their children has been squeezed by the rapid shift of mothers into the paid labour force, by escalating divorce rates and the abandonment of children by their fathers, and by an increase in the number of hours required on the job.'

Much of this new parental time pressure is involuntary, provoked by falling wage rates and escalating housing costs. Many ambitious New Zealand parents work two jobs in order to afford the home they desire. But whatever the reasons, it is bad for children. A 1989 study of fourteen-year-olds in San Diego and Los Angeles found that the more hours children took care of themselves each week, the greater the risk of substance abuse. So-called 'latchkey' children were twice as likely to drink alcohol or take drugs as children under the supervision of an adult after school.

Lesley Max says there is a widespread conviction among those working professionally in areas of health, education, welfare and justice, that many children are harmed by their parents' not possessing the skills to be reasonably competent caregivers, and that effective education for parenthood is vital in order to reduce damage to children, and give them an equitable start in life. She argues that the competence of parents is more critical in New Zealand than in some other countries, because of the greater responsibility parents in this country bear for their children's health.

Schools are suffering from parental indifference towards discipline. A recent editorial in *The Press* noted that it should not be the responsibility of schools to ensure that children can accept the discipline that necessarily accompanies learning: 'That is a task for parents, many of whom seem to have given up challenging the mores of their children's peer group. What is clear is not only that some parents have abdicated responsibility for disciplining their children . . . but [they] resent anyone else taking it on.'

UNICEF says the failure to invest either public resources or private time in the raising of children has left youngsters fending for themselves, and coping more or less badly with the difficult business of growing up in the 1990s: 'True, many children continue to be raised in supportive communities by thoughtful, attentive parents; but looming larger is the overall drift, in both government policy and private adult choices, towards blighting youngsters and stunting their potential. An anti-child spirit is loose in these lands.'

In contrast, the negative trends have not extended to continental Europe or Japan. In the traditionally Catholic countries of southern Europe, families and communities have remained strong enough to continue to provide a supportive environment for raising children, despite some slippage over the last decade. And in the welfare states of Scandinavia, comprehensive and aggressive social policies have compensated for family disintegration and created conditions that allow children to flourish. What these nations share is a wider and deeper vision of collective but costly responsibility for children.

UNICEF has urged countries like New Zealand and the United States to invest more in education: 'Schools can and should do more to prepare youngsters for productive employment, but they will continue to fall short of the mark unless those societies also support parents and give them the time and resources to do better by their children. The education system cannot compensate for the tasks overburdened parents no longer perform . . . Overall, the home is almost twice as powerful as the school in determining student achievement at age fourteen.'

The welfare of children is also being jeopardised by burgeoning divorce rates, sharp increases in out-of-wedlock births, and a striking rise in the number of fatherless households. Deadbeat fathers should pay. The economic harm to children from the divorce of their parents arises from the fact that fathers generally earn more than mothers, but in most cases the children remain with the mothers after divorce.

There is also growing international evidence that the breakup of a marriage can trigger severe behavioural problems among children. A study of more than 700 families by the New York Psychiatric Institute found that youngsters who attempted suicide differed little from those who did not, in terms of age, income, race and religion, but they were much more likely to live in 'non-intact family settings' and to have minimal contact with their fathers. A study by Columbia University found that students who lived without their fathers tended to underperform at school, compared with students from homes with the fathers present.

Children, according to Lesley Max, have become 'the bullets in an ideological-political war waged by adults over the shape and function of the family'. She warns that New Zealand has become so 'tolerant' that it is approaching a stage where the word 'normal' has no meaning other than to denote a repressive judgmentalism: 'It should be possible to deal charitably and humanely, with full respect for the humanity of each individual, no matter how far from the norm that person may be in some attribute, and yet retain some image of where the "norm" is.' The pendulum, she says, has swung from judgmentalism to rigorous non-judging.

We were warned in George Orwell's book *1984* of the dangers of 'newspeak' and 'doublespeak'. Orwell wrote of government slogans that said 'War is Peace', 'Freedom in Slavery' and 'Ignorance is Strength'. Saddam Hussein must have read the book, because he recently told his people that if the Americans came back he would give them another thrashing. When I read *1984* as a teenager, I thought government and big business could control the information age and thus control people. I was wrong. The opposite has happened. The information age, faxes, video cameras and mobile telephones helped the liberation of Eastern Europe by showing the failures of Marxism. It was the faxes, mobile phones and hand-held video cameras that told the world about Tiananmen Square.

Confucius said, 'If language is not used rightly, then what is said is not what is meant. If what is said is not what is meant, then that which ought to be done is left undone. If it remains undone, morals and art will be corrupted. If morals and art are corrupted, justice will go awry. And if justice goes awry, the people will stand about in helpless confusion.'

Words are important. The old cliché 'Sticks and stones may break my bones but words will never hurt me' is untrue. Misuse of words can cause sticks and stones to be thrown. Sensitivity is welcome. It is civilised behaviour. But we have reached a stage where people can no longer express themselves for fear of offence. Decouple people from their language and you promote insecurity and backlash.

This nonsense must stop. No government has a right to rewire children because it believes their 'neutral values' will produce the kind of citizen of which they approve. The so-called new Moscow man to be produced by the Soviets failed miserably. So did the child warriors of the Maoist cultural revolution, but not before ruining millions of lives and setting China back a generation.

Parents and children are unsettled and confused by these changes. People need the security and comfort of institutions that have stood the test of time. Let's slow down and reverse the hijacking of our cultural values, our language and institutions.

We need a long, in-depth debate leading to a social consensus about these issues. There needs to be an ethical and moral commission that can report to Parliament on all these issues. It can be done within a year.

We ought not to make changes without taking a deep breath and thinking about the implications. In-vitro fertilisation and adoption are cases in point. How many parents have been asked for their views? There is a case pending in the US where a sperm donor, years later, is being taken to court by the child he played a part in creating. Has that child the right to know who its parent was; any right to the father's estate? I simply don't know. And I don't want, as a politician, to have to make decisions like this on my own. We need the views of all interested parties. My views are not that important, nor are the views of other politicians. We can only move with the acceptance of parents.

The issue is not whether we discriminate against people on the basis of gender, or whether or not they accept the values of the majority. There should be no discrimination, and those who do discriminate should be shunned and legislated against. But there is a difference between anti-discrimination and values-neutral education, laws and policies. The intolerance is coming now from people who were once victims. The old values were about tolerance, and they were correct. Vice is not an equal-value neutral position. Good parents create good children. The state must be the last resort, a helpful supporter, not a replacement.

Every child is born innocent and good. What happens next is up to their parents, and the rest of us have a duty to help. That's what this book is about.

six

Growing Together

ONE OF THE REASONS I wrote this book was the fear I had that the agenda needed for the children of the poor would be captured by the tired old Left, those who could use these problems to smuggle back discredited theories and economic models of controls, subsidies, and protectionism; the promise of a better past when coal was king. Our modern open economy, they will correctly claim, works for 80 percent of the people but not the 20 percent at the bottom. Their solution will be to abolish the success of the 80 percent, as though that will help those who have borne the brunt of the restructuring and internationalisation of the New Zealand economy.

It is true that we have failed to make our economy work for enough New Zealanders. But it is equally true that the open economic model has delivered more jobs, opportunities and security to more people than any system yet devised. Nations that embrace trade win; those that don't, lose. As I explained in the Introduction, countries that have embraced full trade have doubled the real incomes of their workers in a remarkably short time. That is the undeniable lesson of economic history. Sure, some of these countries started from a low economic base, but if it is easy to produce a dramatic improvement from such a position, why didn't it happen earlier, under Marxist economics?

We just need to inch up minimum wages and conditions, and to expand the success of our economy to include more people. To do so will take hard, calculated management. We must embrace the international marketplace and drive our advantages home. It can be done.

New Zealand accounts for barely 0.06 percent of the world's

population and our slice of the world's trade is a miniscule 0.27 percent. Like it or not, the world economy will always drive us; we will never drive it. Understanding and accepting the reality of the global economy is a key first step in shaping our response.

Our living standards – how we eat, our entertainment trends, what we wear, even what we believe – are frequently beyond our control. When Batman mania swept New Zealand, it happened because of movies made in America. The Teenage Mutant Ninja Turtles and Transformers crazes among children, for example, were not local phenomena. They stemmed from imported television programmes and movies that encouraged children to go out and buy imported toys. Fashion shows in Paris help dictate world demand for our wool. Health food fads in California can help or hinder our export industry. When Meryl Streep goes on television in California and says there are insecticides on apples, apple consumption slumps 30 percent. Downstream, that could make someone in Hawke's Bay unemployed. But if she had said New Zealand apples didn't have such insecticides, our sales would have climbed. We have to ensure New Zealand is a benefactor rather than a victim of global circumstances.

As Helmut Schmidt, the outstanding West German Social Democratic chancellor put it, 'national strategies are anachronistic in our present-day world'. He points out that for small countries such as Holland or Luxembourg it is outdated nonsense to even think of a purely national economic policy, a purely national foreign policy or a purely national security policy. Even the super-economies of Japan and the United States cannot by their own national means alone achieve their economic goals, their political goals or external security.

A country can no longer realistically expect to boost its economy in isolation from global realities, as the Mitterand government in France found to its peril a few years ago. Mitterand tried to inflate his economy out of recession, but 'slippage' meant more imports from Italy and Germany. New spending did not create the jobs in France as expected. Purely national policies cannot work in isolation, and this is equally true of the great nations as it is of the small.

There needs to be strategic planning and partnership. There need be no contradiction between free markets and planning.

Collective capitalism is really a partnership, a compact, a growth agreement between government, business and the great institutions of research and education.

Management guru Peter Drucker argues that the world economy is not changing: it has *already* changed, in its foundations and in its structure, and in all probability the change is irreversible. Within the last decade or so, three fundamental changes have occurred in the very fabric of the world economy. The primary-products economy has come uncoupled from the industrial economy. In the industrial economy itself, production has come uncoupled from employment: growth does not always mean more jobs. In fact, in some industries job shedding is a pre-requisite for new growth. And capital movements rather than trade (in both goods and services) have become the driving force of the world economy. Drucker says that although capital movements and trade in goods and services have not quite become uncoupled, the link has become loose and, worse, unpredictable.

These changes, he argues, are permanent rather than cyclical: 'We may never understand what caused them. The causes of economic change are rarely simple. It may be a long time before economic theorists accept that there have been fundamental changes, and longer still before they adapt their theories to account for them. Above all, they will surely be most reluctant to accept that it is the world economy in control, rather than the macro-economics of the nation state on which most economic theory will exclusively focus.'

The important message for New Zealand is that no nation can hope to survive by ignoring this growing global reality, unless they want to have Albanian or North Korean standards and styles of living. In Richard John Seddon's time, coal was king. In Michael Joesph Savage's time it was diesel. Now it is communications, information and education. The concept of the global village, advocated by Marshall McLuhan two decades ago, is now a reality.

I saw it illustrated during a visit to Papua New Guinea. A senior public servant showing us around said his father had never met a white man until the age of 50. He, in turn, had been educated at an Australian university, and lived in a village where his son communicated with a pen friend in America via computer and satellite. He smiled and said, 'I have one foot in the stone age and one foot in the space age.'

We are in the post-industrial economy, the information age. During the industrial age, the chief inputs were steel, energy, paper and sweat. Now the chief inputs are ideas, information and intellectual property. 'Information' workers and the new 'gold-collar' workers of banking and capital markets are already outnumbering traditional blue-collar employees. Japanese experts say that they will increase manufacturing output within twenty years and cut blue-collar workers by 25 to 40 percent. A kilogram of fibre optics can shift more information than a tonne of copper wire. In 1862 the cost of sending a single word by international telegram was equal to a year's pay for a worker. Now, the equivalent of 15 minutes' work pays to send a full-page fax anywhere in the world.

Technology, research and development has worked. Manufacturing production in the United States grew by approximately 40 percent during the 1980s, but five million blue-collar jobs disappeared. New jobs and new employment have risen dramatically, but not in traditional blue-collar areas. New products demand less in the way of mineral resources and other raw materials, but more labour in the form of information workers.

A summary, in two words, of what it takes to be internationally competitive is 'constant innovation'. That means constantly creating new products and new processes in a way that reflects evolving buyer needs. You can't achieve this by getting government subsidies and protection. In fact, it boomerangs. You achieve and maintain international competitiveness by being exposed to the cold, harsh winds of competition and by having a partnership made up of business, the workforce, researchers and government.

Our role models for seizing and exploiting opportunities live around our shared Pacific Rim. Asian economies have undergone a mind-boggling turnaround in less than half a lifetime. Forty years ago Japan was still recovering from the horrors of war. Half of its workforce was still in the paddy fields, with the remainder in factories that were barely 10 percent as efficient as those in America. Hong Kong and Singapore were busy ports, but little more. And now? Japan is now one of the world's industrial superpowers, while the four economic tigers of Asia – South Korea, Taiwan, Singapore and Hong Kong – have pushed through the fastest industrial revolution the world has ever seen. Thailand, Malaysia, Indonesia and the southern economic zone of China will soon be nudging at their heels. Within a generation China will have a GNP wealth equal to the combined economies of Japan and the United States.

Forty years ago New Zealanders would have regarded most Singaporeans as coolies. Today, the incomes of Singaporeans and the citizens of Hong Kong have overtaken those of New Zealanders. The rise in Asian prosperity is outpacing us. In Japan, the average income is double that of New Zealanders. Experts predict that by the year 2000 there will be 110 million people in the ASEAN countries, China, and Taiwan with incomes equal to or better than those of New Zealanders.

What I am saying in this chapter will jar with many good social liberals. It's designed to. Many who share my views about the state of New Zealand's children will say the anwer is to throw the economy into reverse gear. Some say our relative economic success is actually the problem. They oppose an open economic strategy.

What is it about trade liberalisation that attracts such public abuse? There is a mutant strain of leftist thought that still believes private enterprise, trade and business is wicked. Some, like the old Social Crediters of the Alliance, even argue that it is a global conspiracy. After the Wall Street crash of the 1920s the United States threw up trade barriers, exacerbating the world depression that brought misery to millions. A growing, free, world economy is a matter of political, economic and military security.

Our great international institutions need also to reflect the new age. The economic institutions created at Bretton Woods after the Second World War – the IMF, World Bank and the GATT – were designed to complement in global economic policy the political work of the United Nations. It was hoped that a system of global Keynesianism could operate through these financial institutions. That vision has been blurred but not yet blinded, and it ought to be acknowledged that these institutions have given the world a longer and more consistent period of growth.

But the reality of the 1990s is that these institutions no longer reflect the needs of the new global economy. They need reform. When these institutions were established, Japan and Germany were shattered by war. Politicians still thought in terms of national economies and food security. Jet transport was barely invented. There were no faxes, satellites or instant communication systems. It just was not possible to live in New Zealand and work in Wall Street, New York or Sydney as some 'global' New Zealanders now do.

Global trade was one of the two principles both Karl Marx and Adam Smith said could unite nations and peoples. The Americans now send investment missions to Japan, the United Kingdom and Europe. Developing countries know these days that if they want jobs and the latest medical advances, education and top technology, they need investment. Listen to leaders like Nelson Mandela, Lee Kwan Yew, or even Aleksander Kwashiewski, the new communist-backed President of Poland. The irony is that in the northern hemisphere it is the Right, like Buchanan in the United States, and ultra-nationalists like Le Pen in France, who run the anti-investment anti-foreigner line.

The real danger has been of losing momentum towards a global deal and the outbreak of regional trade deals like the European Community and the North American Free Trade Treaty. New Zealand and Australia worried about being left out. What if Japan and Korea did a bilateral deal with the United States on agriculture? We would lose hundreds of thousands of jobs. Thus, the Asia-Pacific Economic Co-operation Council (APEC) was formed. At the first meeting at which I represented New Zealand, I feared a new de facto currency economic zone based on the US dollar, the yen and the deutschmark. This has not happened, although regional agreements now exist in ways that can hopefully accelarate free and fair trade.

The World Trade Organisation has worked for New Zealand already. Japan, Europe and Korea have opened many of their markets for products such as apples and beef. Opponents of an open economic strategy claim it exploits the poor of developing countries, as well as the poor in New Zealand. We know that the people of the Philippines don't want handouts: they want access for their products. What is true for our kiwifruit, sheepmeat and fish is equally true for the rice of Thailand, the sugar of the Philippines and the manufactured products of Malaysia. One dollar's worth of transfer to developing countries through higher agricultural prices is equivalent to between $2.20 and $14 in foreign aid. A dollar of well-spent aid can raise incomes by between $1.20 and $2.00. Compare this to the increase in income of between $4.50 and $27.30 made possible by every dollar transferred to developing countries (excluding the oil exporters) through an increase in world agricultural prices. Julius Nyerere expressed it this way: 'It is as true for a nation as it is for a village shopkeeper that the poverty of your potential customers is a limitation upon your own affluence.'

Those who say that the World Trade Organisation denies the sovereignty of nations are wrong. Each government must sign up and agree to the programmes. It is a contract between nations to treat each other equally. It enhances the sovereignty of small and weak nations. Japan, or the United States, cannot ignore or push around small nations. They cannot do side deals and give each other preferences. For a generation New Zealand trade ministers were humilated by going to Brussels and Paris, not to negotiate for butter and sheepmeat access to Europe, but to lobby. Now we are independent; our trade rights are guaranteed by international law. When the French stopped some of our exports because of the *Rainbow Warrior* incident, we were able to win the case using World Trade Organisation rules. Small nations need civilised rules of conduct.

Some have suggested that the trade deal works against human rights. What nonsense. The United Nations has had members that have been communists and fascists – should we encourage their expulsion? The only major nations that are not World Trade Organisation members in the Pacific Rim are China, North Korea and Burma. They also have among the worst human rights records in our region. We should encourage these nations to open up, join the world, and respect universal human, economic and political rights by global trade as well as political resolutions.

There are more than 150 million children in Third World countries working in conditions and for pay that constitutes a new form of slavery. The situation of a child forced to make carpets in Pakistan is clearly different from that of a child working on a newspaper round or picking fruit in an OECD country. Many of the countries guilty of this new form of slavery are not members of the World Trade Organisation, but some are. Child labour ought to be considered in the next round of negotiations.

More than 60 percent of New Zealand jobs are related to open investment, trade and tourism. And 70 per cent of our trade is with Asia-Pacific Economic Co-operation members. A larger percentage of New Zealand's economy is based on exports than is the case for Japan, the US or Germany. When I was born, 90 per cent of our trade went to Britain. Critics have said I care more about trade and business than people. What 1960s hippie nonsense. Trade is about jobs and profits. It generates tax for health and education. We can't advance the cause of families and children if there's no wealth to share.

I don't really believe New Zealanders have a problem with the goal of more jobs, a fairer society or a sustainable economy. Our differences are over means, not objectives. And that implies we already have an enormous consensus. What we have to do is convince people that our health system and our ability to abolish foodbanks or educate our children is based on maintaining and growing our economy in the world marketplace. The best hope for the children of the poor is a global strategy accepting that truth. That's how countries like Singapore, Taiwan, Austria, Germany, Korea, Japan – societies devastated by war – can now boast that their children have a better future than ours. They have learnt the harsh realities of the global economy.

New Zealand is rich in resources, and even richer in opportunities. Why is it that these other nations have done better than us – in terms of living standards, infant mortality and educational achievement – when they seemingly have so little? Do we care less for our children than they do? Of course not. It is all a question of leadership, a vision, direction and drive. Other nations have such leadership.

seven

Towards a More Civil Society

COMMENTATORS BEMOAN the decline of the family and the rejection of civil order. The public are constantly shocked by the arrogant disregard for community values and civil norms displayed by young people who, without remorse, guilt or shame, commit mindless crimes of violence. Family satbility has been diminished by changing work habits and the civic desert of suburban sprawl and urban decay.

What has happened? I have written earlier of the decline of social and urban solidarity between neighbours. Civil society has evolved, through its institutions and culture, written and unwritten law, certain acceptable sets of values and limits of behaviour. Religion played a role. It set the boundaries. Treating your neighbour as you would like to be treated, honouring marriage and intergenerational respect, duty to family and society: these profound principles were endorsed by all great religions. People knew what was right and what was wrong. We didn't need a policeman or a court to mediate for us. That is, most of us. In a rural society we depended on each other on hay-baling day, to run the co-op or manage the school. We shared the same values, jobs and problems.

Law evolved to arbitrate when co-operation failed. When different parties refused to work out their differences and problems there had to be some sanction against those who refused to co-operate. Third-party enforcement became the solution. Parties in conflict surrendered individual rights to another stronger authority to enforce the rules. Their reward was the mutual confidence necessary to civil life and order. Law and order was thus seen as the solution to strife. The monarchy once held all the power and, endowed with a 'God-given' gift of authority, ruled. The 'good' king shared and was fair. The 'bad' king served special interests, normally his own and those of the ruling class. The people eventually expanded their power through co-operatives, unions, political action and popular franchise.

The whole idea of civilisation was to progress and expand freedom, both materially and socially. Anarchy was once almost an acceptable response to the excesses of political power. The state was not – and still is not – always the friend of freedom and the people. ACT is the closest New Zealand has come to an anarchist party. Its zealous supporters believe that if the state disappears so will the problems.

The nation state evolved as the solution to problems that individuals, tribes and feuding princes couldn't resolve. Internationalism has, in turn, grown in significance as the solution to border disputes between nations. It is true that societies where social cohesion functions without formal rules and rigid or violent enforcement by the state do better. The successes of Germany and Japan, both economically and socially, are examples.

The larger the police force, and the more detailed and intrusive the laws of a nation, the more expensive the transaction costs of monitoring and enforcing civil agreements. Take as an example the medical system in the United States, where each doctor must pay $100,000 per year just for insurance against litigation. The United States has five times as many lawyers per capita than New Zealand. It is said that in a small American town one lawyer will starve, but two will both make a good living.

Civil society rests on responsibility and co-operation as much as law and its enforcement. Failure is costly. One economist, Oliver Williamson, writes of 'transaction costs' as a barrier to economic progress. Such costs reduce a nation's competitiveness. Environmental pressure has led to new forms of institutions and laws to manage scarce resources. Political support to succeed in practice is necessary to promote the political willpower to pass such legislation.

Common values are underestimated as an economic and social good. It is no good one nation having a clean air or clean river policy, if another country upstream or upwind does not. The same can be said of trading and immigration policies. Internationalism is the force of the future, just as nationalism was a source of good and bad this century.

Co-operation is the key to success. Countries, companies and individuals who litigate, sue or blacklist in frustration at the failure of another party to co-operate, join in the common failure to resolve a problem.

What builds a strong civil society? The answer is its institutions, customs and culture. That is social capital. Social trust is the expectation that your neighbour, competitor, teacher, your daughter's fiancée, the courts, police and the suppliers of goods you purchase, whether it's a second-hand car or electricity, will do the right thing. That they will act in accord with civil and honest behaviour. It is integrity and honour, based on common values.

Where that social trust is broken, civil society retreats. When a politician lies to the people by promising no surcharge, no student fees, and no new taxes, he betrays trust and shows by his example that civil order can be broken. The same is true of a policeman who has taken a bribe, a teacher who has given up, or a parent who is more interested in housie than his or her children's education. If the very wealthy appear to pay no tax while the poor battle on, it is seen as immoral and wrong. It breaks social trust and betrays our common values.

Civil society is about reciprocity: treating others as we would wish to be treated. We will baby-sit for you because you will watch our house when we are on holiday. It combines short-term altruism with long-term interest. In his book *Making Democracy Work*, Robert Putham writes: 'Networks of civic engagement increase the potential costs to a defector in any individual transaction. Opportunism puts at risk the benefits he expects to receive from all other transactions in which he is currently engaged, as well as the benefits from future transactions. Compatriots who interact in many social contexts are apt to develop strong norms of acceptable behaviour and to convey their mutual expectations to one another in many reinforcing encounters. These norms are reinforced by the network of relationships that depend on the establishment of a reputation for keeping promises and accepting the norms of the local community regarding behaviour.

'Networks of civic engagement facilitate communication and improve the flow of information about the trustworthiness of individuals. Networks of civic engagement allow reputations to be transmitted and refined . . . Trust and co-operation depend on reliable information about the past behaviour and present interest of potential partners, while uncertainty reinforces dilemmas of collective action. Thus, other things being equal, the greater the communication (both direct and indirect) among participants, the greater the mutual trust and the easier they will find it to co-operate.'

Putham examines how parts of Italy with strong civic networks are successful and where such networks are not powerful, these provinces fall behind and fail.

The politics of rights, not duties and responsibilities, have flourished throughout Western societies since the 1960s. The crazy Right argue that individualism and self-interest should be the only rules, while the extreme Left seek to destroy the values and institutions developed over generations to maintain social and civic order.

We live in a world corrupted by individualism. Margaret Thatcher summed it up by saying, 'There is no such thing as society.' The world is also perverted by liberal values that confuse liberalism with a licence to do anything that pleases you. The power-mad Left and populists like Sir Robert Muldoon tried to deny individualism for the common good (as they defined it). William Blake, in *Jerusalem*, says, 'The general good is the plea of the scoundrel, hypocrite and flatterer.' Having failed to control the economy through a flawed concept of state ownership, some now want to control people through political correctness and social engineering.

Rousseau, in *The Social Contract*, warned against the worship of the state, which he said was not the act of a free citizen, but of the subject or slave. Plato spoke of an ideal republic where the citizen was so well educated and trained as a citizen 'so to have embodied in himself the principle of duty in general, that no enforcement against him of particular duty, nor system of sanction, would be required, nor anti-civic act, wilful or inadvertent, to be committed by him'.

Equipping people to be productive citizens is also a fundamental duty of our education system. Teaching civic duty and civil obligations as well as 'rights' must now be central to educating for life. The decadent Americanisation of our values system, based on their founding fathers' promise that every citizen has a right 'to pursue happiness', is only half the story. The other half is about responsibilities and duty to oneself and the community. Civil engagement and popular participation is more than the two-minute exercise of ticking a name and a party once every three years.

However, democracy is the most basic component of civil society. It is no historic mistake that democratic states with free markets do better. It is no historic fluke of nature that democratic trade unions and free intitutions are a consistent part of economic and social success. It is no accident that the historic changes in Eastern Europe began with trade unions, from the pivotal role of Solidarity in Poland to the attempted coup in Moscow, which was ended with the threat of a general strke.

The president of a new Czechoslovakia, Vaclav Havel, said that political repression in Eastern Europe robbed those nations of a healthy civic life and worthwhile public institutions: 'Trade unions, democratic involvement and management of our health systems, public ownership of our energy system, are important to our life, our way of doing things. Eastern Europe's problems were not only problems of shortages of private investment, but because public investment and structures, from phones to roads to schools, were in disrepair.'

The West had a better environmental record not only because the market was better than the state, but because democratic civil engagement by the people via politicians had demanded it. The green protest movement plays a valid role in a democracy. Public officials and industrial managers in the East were free from public pressure and scrutiny. The cruel orphanages of Romania and China could not survive an exposé by the news media of a free society.

There is no civil engagement or protest movement in totalitarian societies. The lessons of Eastern Europe were not that we must fear and dread government, public and collective engagement, but that we need a democratic public life built on solid and sensible civic engagement. It was democracy that fostered social movements which drew attention to aspects of capitalism that didn't work – the New Deal in the United States, the welfare state in New Zealand, the growth of green movements and the desire for equity in issues of gender and race.

Our modern society is also seeing the shrinking of civil engagement and civil society. The sanctions against uncivil behaviour do not work if the family and church decline. They are the structures that have produced responsible and reasonable behaviour. Third parties such as the police, the courts and schools are being conscripted more and more to deal with these failures, and are then blamed for not doing enough for our collective failures.

Policies that support families and civic engagement are good. Policies that weaken them are bad. The costs of families falling apart are enormous, and threaten a backlash against the whole concept of the welfare state, which is seen by its critics to encourage the separation of families. The welfare state is a 'third party' attempt to intervene on behalf of society to solve a problem before it explodes and hurts its immediate victim and others. It is a moral and economic force for good. The welfare state does save some beaten women from terrible poverty and their children from second-class citizenship, if run properly. But it has also provided a hammock for some, rather than a springboard out of trouble.

Civil engagement and popular participation can be brought back to life, giving new meaning to citizens and more control over their lives, while at the same time building up more secure, enjoyable and healthy communities. People have a basic need to be part of something larger than themselves, whether through a trade union or church congregation, or even membership of a bowling club.

In an earlier chapter I wrote of a lawn-mowing, football-playing democracy. That is not as trite as it might sound. Societies with strong networks of clubs and organisations have less crime, stronger families, more productive businesses and happier people. We need to re-invent these traditions and give new life to this traditionally Kiwi way of doing things. The fourth

Labour government created more than 20,000 neighbourhood watch groups, encouraging people to work with their neighbours to combat crime. It worked. Where these groups got together, crime dropped. Such initiatives also have a wider spinoff for the community. They help to cure loneliness, and strengthen families and communities.

We are wasting too many people. Why not encourage those in retirement, or close to retirement, to help us all out? Many do now: it is predominantly the elderly and late middle-aged who run the raffles, meals on wheels and the clubs. There are many organisations that have at their centre a core group of professionals, many with military or police backgrounds: the Red Cross, fire service, Coast Guard, St Johns, surf-lifesavers. They form an invaluable network of volunteers. These clubs and organisations are a large part of what holds our society together. Why not encourage some people to retire early, give their job to a young person and then pay them a little to help out in the community to reorganise and give life to our civic organisations? Let's say to young unemployed people, many of whom are at risk, that if you can't find a job we want you to help organise and work for St Johns, or a local club or beautification society, for a few days a week. Initially it would be an invitation. Later it could become a condition for receiving the the unemployment benefit or DPB.

Much of our working, sexual, social and family lives can be summed up as 'participation without commitment'. There is a vast army that participates in great All Black and America's Cup victories and telethons, but too often as an audience of one or two. People want to be neighbours and want to be involved, but do not know how, or they fear personal engagement. That is why soap operas and talkbacks are so popular. It is participation without commitment.

As a member of Parliament, I have been privileged to live other people's lives and problems. Sometimes you think people do not care; that it would be easy to just force them to pay their taxes, and then when in government buy your way out of trouble by handing out money to those in need. That's the easy, lazy way to govern. I do not believe we have reached the compassion fatigue stage, despite the popular political market to attack the welfare state.

In the past two years I have worked on two cases in particular that have ignited public support and generosity.

One involved a single mum. She had been a schoolgirl in a conservative rural town. She got pregnant and kept the child while at school. The child had Down's syndrome. Don't you admire her already? Later she married a man who turned out to be violent and abusive. She separated from him, and struggled through university until, in the last year of her degree, she thought she would have to toss it in because she couldn't afford day-care costs and university fees. The case went public. People sent money to the newspaper office; even a visiting tourist went to the paper and made a donation. The woman ended up with more money than she needed.

In the second case a man in my area had lost his wife to cancer. He had two healthy children, and one very sick little boy. The boy was profoundly disabled, mentally and physically, and needed 24-hour care. The man was told to go on the DPB. But he was running a small business and was employing six people. The government wouldn't pay out $400 a week for a caregiver, so he was looking at closing his business down. If that happened the taxpayer would be out of pocket to the tune of $5000 a week in dole payments and lost tax revenue. The public was outraged and showered the man with flowers, love and support. Eventually common sense prevailed: the government backed down over the bad publicity and agreed to provide payment for a caregiver.

What have these two cases got in common? Do they prove people don't care any more? No. They prove the opposite. People still hate injustice and stupid short-sighted bureaucratic indifference. They are inspired by people who help themselves. And therein lies the answer. We need to provide systems and opportunities for people to help themselves. We, the state, will help – but we want you to help yourselves. Unless we change we will suffer the worst aspects of capitalist culture, where some people eat food prepared for dogs and others buy dogs, not for the pleasure of man's best friend, but to protect their homes from man's worst enemy: man.

Even if you judge the worth of an individual or a society using the most venal cost-accounting criteria, my argument is that you must come down on the side of the poor and the family. Even if you judge a nation by its terms of trade rather than its art and music.

Lee Kwan Yew, the Singaporean leader, once warned a group of visiting ministers that the future economic race would be between Confucian capitalism and European-style Christian capitalism. He told us that the Confucian model would win through because of its commitment to family, education, community and its all-abiding respect for tradition, education and the elderly. The West, in contracting out the responsibility for children and the elderly to the state, would lose the economic war. This will only happen if we let it happen.

The ultimate betrayal of the young would be to build up more debt, allow the economic dysentry of inflation to take hold, and to allow our precious public health and education systems to perish.

eight

An Agenda for the Children of the Poor

Economy

To provide the wealth needed to save the children of New Zealand's poor, we need a strong economy. Our ability to raise education standards, improve the health status of the nation's children and remove the need for food banks will be based on expanding our economy. A reckless, reactionary reversal from an open market will not help children; nor will it create wealth or jobs. It will do the opposite. The debate is about distribution of wealth and opportunity, not its creation.

The new government should:

Accept with confidence the reality of the global marketplace, and acknowledge that New Zealand cannot expect to boost its economy in isolation from global realities. As an isolated island state, it is most important for New Zealand to capitalise on the opportunities for jobs and growth through international trade. Singapore and South Korea's infant mortality rates and social conditions have improved almost in direct relationship to their economic success. We will create more jobs and generate more tax revenue by getting one percent of the United States and European Union milk, beef or football jersey markets than we will by creating an economic island of tariffs and protectionism and guaranteeing ourselves 100 percent of the New Zealand market.

Reject attempts to use the problems facing the children of the poor to smuggle back discredited theories and economic models of controls, subsidies, and protectionism. It is true that we have failed to make our economy work for enough New Zealanders. But it is equally true that the open economic model has delivered more jobs, opportunities and security to more people than any system yet devised. This is not to say that it can't be improved.

Promote strategic planning and partnerships between government, business, the workforce and the institutions of research and education. There need be no contradiction between the free market and planning for growth. All companies have corporate plans and work to a vision or statement of goals. So should a nation. Industry groups should be encouraged to work together inside the discipline of the global market to promote New Zealand, and its products and services. Self-interest will bind them together, not subsidies or regulations or ministerial edict. The government should become their best friend.

Families and communities

The family in all its forms has been the basic unit in every society, every civilisation, every great religion throughout the ages. Policies and programmes that support families are good. Those that split families are bad. People should be urged to play their part in building a more interesting and better New Zealand. It will require vision, enthusiasm, energy and the courage to make mistakes.

The new government should rebuild civil society by:

Slowing down and reversing the hijacking of our cultural values, our language and institutions by those who are seeking to impose an extreme brand of political correctness on the rest of us. This nonsense must stop. Nobody has the right to re-wire children because they believe their 'neutral values' will produce the kind of citizen of which they approve. Parents and children are unsettled and confused by these changes. People need the security and comfort of institutions that have stood the test of time. Our grandparents were right when they produced co-operative structures to support families.

Setting up an ethical and moral commission that can report to Parliament within a year on these issues. Politicians need guidance, and can only move with the acceptance of parents, whose views are paramount. Let's teach ethics and say what is right and wrong.

Encouraging new forms of civil engagement and popular participation, which will give new meaning to citizens and more control over their lives, while at the same time building up more secure, enjoyable and healthy communities. People have a basic need to be part of something larger than themselves. Rebuild and re-invent civil responsibility and civil society.

Encouraging some people to retire early, give their job to a young person, and then pay them a little to help out in the community, to reorganise and give life to our civic organisations. We also need to re-create the apprenticeship system.

Giving young unemployed people, many of whom are at risk, the opportunity to help in community organisations such as St Johns, or a local club or beautification society for a few days a week. Initially it would be an invitation. Later it could become a condition for receiving the the unemployment benefit or DPB.

Education

Everything we do in the name of developing the nation, making it economically strong, a decent place to live and grow old in, we do in the name of New Zealand's future. 'The future' is just another phrase for children. The challenge to us all is not to betray the faith and the hope our young people have in us. Giving them an education that will equip them to take on the world is probably the most precious gift they will ever receive. We must teach responsibilties as well as rights.

The new government should:

Take a wider approach to education. Children will be more successful at school if they are healthy and well fed. Eliminating health problems such as glue ear will be a good start, and will have a positive spin-off for the education of our young. If we fail in this, we fail everywhere.

Ensure there is more home-based support for parents and young children.

Significantly increase the budget for early childhood education subsidies so that group sizes can be reduced and standards raised.

Provide extra money to accommodate growing early childhood education rolls, and to tackle maintenance and building needs.

Recognise preschool workers as first teachers, and raise their standards and conditions.

Set up an equity funding system to help compensate for the lack of resources available to low-income communities. All areas are not created equal.

Remove the barriers to setting up kohanga reo and Pacific Island language groups.

Provide extra funding or the Correspondence School's early childhood programme and mobile kindergartens.

Restore the funds cut from school operating grants since 1990.

Double equity funding for schools in poorer areas.

Guarantee the right of every child to attend their local school.

Scrap bulk funding of teachers' salaries and the voucher scheme for private schools.

Build new schools to meet population needs, and immediately carry out the repairs needed to bring existing buildings up to quality standards.

Reduce class sizes, particularly in junior classes and poorer schools.

Stop truancy, and ensure that no child is expelled or suspended from school without firm and complete follow-up.

Set up a central database to ensure students no longer drop out of the system.

Provide core funding for teaching English to speakers of other languages, so that the learning of these students and their classmates is not held back.

Support pay parity between primary and secondary teachers. Teachers need to be properly rewarded for the critical roles they play in the economy, and funds should also be provided to train teachers and counsellors to help children at risk and reduce truancy and disruptive behaviour in class.

Increase funding for Maori education at all levels, including kohanga reo, kura kaupapa and wananga. More money should also be invested to increase the number of Maori teachers and teachers competent in te reo and nga tikanga Maori.

Ensure nobody in New Zealand is denied access to tertiary education because of inability to pay. Student allowances should be increased to the level of the unemployment benefit, and should be given to sixteen- and seventeen-year-olds in full-time study.

Widen access to allowances, and progressively abolish the means test on parental income.

Lower student fees to $1000 per year for all full-time courses, so that young people can choose the course that suits their interests and abilities, rather than their pockets.

Raise the income threshold before repayment of students loans is required, from the present $14,300 per annum to $25,000 a year. Interest should not be charged while students are still studying. We should make it easier for former students to clear their debts by matching dollar for dollar any payment above the minimum required.

Assist with student job creation so that students can earn real money over the summer break.

Develop policies which encourage a levelling effect between information haves and have-nots. We need to consider initiatives which increase computer ownership in low-income households, promote development of public access network services, and fund network literacy programmes through schools, public libraries and adult education programmes. Every school ought to be on the Internet by the turn of the century.

Health

Improving the health of New Zealand's children and young people is the top priority. It is the most basic human right. Truby King, the founder of Plunket, was a visionary who thought laterally, beyond the narrow confines of institutions. We need visionaries like him again, to look out across the next 50 years and see ways to preserve and enhance the health of New Zealand's children.

The new government should begin a nationwide crusade to:

Ensure that home-based health visits are provided for all mothers of new-born babies.

Boost funds for agencies providing such services, for example, Plunket and Tipa Ora, so that the number of home visits children receives in their first five years can be increased. Plunket should be properly funded from a single source.

Investigate ways to advance the Plunket system and marry it to today's high technology.

Ensure that no child under five has to pay to go to the doctor.

Remove standard charges for prescriptions for children under five, and reduce charges for older children.

Ensure that district health services should work with schools to identify the immediate need for school food, or other programmes, to improve child nutritional levels.

Ensure that parent support services are offered to families identified as being under serious stress. These services should provide ongoing home support tailored to the specific needs of the family. Family-care services which offer community-based advice and support to families with older children are also needed. The aim should be to focus on preventing problems occurring which would put the health and wellbeing of the children at risk.

Fund a public media campaign to make drug-taking less romantic and to encourage people to take the health issue more seriously. We must reject soft liberal attitudes to all drugs.

Ensure resources are available for the full range of mental health services that are required for young people, as well as community-based support for patients and carers, counselling and referral services and crisis intervention services.

Create decent shelters for young people who cannot cope or look after themselves. The word 'asylum' need not be a menacing word or mean a place that cruelly represses people. **Continue to fund the development of intensive-care community teams.**

Ensure that no mental health patient is discharged into community care before appropriate services have been put into place for them. Any district health service which is considering discharging such a patient should be required to ensure an agreed care plan has been developed. Community care can work for most if resources are made available and if the concept is not used as a way of saving money or transferring the problem emotionally, financially and socially to the family and the community.

Social security

The welfare state is in need of revolution. We need a massive redirection of resources and a revolution in our thinking because, quite simply, the present system is not working. This new direction is not meant to be reactive or to punish people for their misfortunes. Rather, it accepts the misfortunes in an understanding way and for a short time helps provide a way out, a launching pad to independence, instead of an economic and social prison. The goal must be to make the welfare state a springboard and not a depressing, morale-stripping dead-end hammock.

The new government should:

Raise the standard of living of families on low incomes. The first step should be to raise benefit and family support levels.

Reduce taxes for low-income earners.

Ensure that no young person is left on the dole. Being on the unemployment benefit ought to be a temporary situation, not a permanent one. To put aside a billion and a half dollars each year to pay a few hundred thousand New Zealanders to do nothing is a short-sighted approach. It is the easy, lazy option.

Ensure every young person is offered a choice of education, training, employment or community work. There ought to be a job search allowance for a couple of months, then a ticket to training and re-skilling towards a permanent job in the private workforce. Alternatively, there should be a permanent job in the community workforce, rebuilding New Zealand's infrastructure, creating something positive in the community. Creating such work will be expensive in the short term, if you are only looking at the social welfare budget. But it is not more expensive if you look at the assets that can be built and the tax that can be gathered from having people in the paid workforce, let alone the rich social dividend paid back when families stay together. Another useful option would be military training and upskilling, which could provide some people with a sense of purpose and belonging.

Identify young jobseekers who are at risk of long-term unemployment, so they can receive individual help to ensure they get a job, or continue education or training.

Ensure that young people are eligible for employment programmes after three months rather than the current six months. We should encourage and then insist on co-operation and enrolment into such schemes before the dole is paid.

Raise the minimum youth wage.

Housing

The Kiwi ideal of a lawnmowing, home-owning democracy exists for many, but a large disposed minority is growing, without hope through motivation. A family in their own home is more likely to stay together, teach their kids and fulfill the Kiwi dream.

The new government should:

Keep interest rates down, because they are the biggest long-term cost to home ownership.

Scrap market rents for state houses, along with the profit focus of Housing New Zealand.

Reintroduce a formula for income-related rents, with low-income state tenants paying only a quarter of their net incomes in rent.

Establish a state house-building programme in areas of high housing demand and need.

Provide access to subsidised mortages for low- and modest-income earners, and to others with special housing needs.

Initiate programmes to help people understand the requirements of home ownership, and investigate alternative programmes to help people own their own homes.

Set up a community housing division within the Housing Corporation. It should be responsible for providing appropriate houses to organisations dealing with emergency housing, refuges, services for youth at risk and other groups with special needs.

Crime and justice

Criminals are generally not born: they are made and they are made early in their lives. We need policies which ensure that all children get a decent start, rather than beginning life with attitudes distorted by abuse, neglect and poor role modelling. The need to protect children from abuse and neglect can no longer be ignored. Inter-generational cycles of abuse, neglect and poverty can be broken by effective early intervention. Unless we act now to deal with this problem and the underlying factors leading to a growth in juvenile crime, today's juvenile offenders will become tomorrow's adult career criminals.

The new government should:

Urgently improve the responsiveness of crisis-intervention services for families.

Increase funding for the Children and Young Persons Service, to recognise the increased workload and to provide for improved training of staff. Funding must be maintained at a level sufficient to enable staff to investigate and resolve cases promptly.

Give more help to schools to deal earlier and effectively with disruptive and violent behaviour by children.

Develop positive recreational activities for children from at-risk and disadvantaged families.

Ensure that communities are protected from serious and recidivist offending by a small hard core of violent juvenile offenders, by keeping them in secure custody while efforts are made to change their behaviour.

Adequately resource community-based prevention and rehabilitation programmes with proven records of success.

Develop programmes which encourage prisoners to change their attitude, to develop work skills, work habits and work experience, and to address the cause of their criminal behaviour, such as alcohol and drug addiction and mental disorders.

Ensure there are alternative options to returning youths to the environment, family or peer group which led to their offending in the first place.

Create a new programme with professionally trained foster parents and mentors to which difficult young people can be referred.

Encourage young offenders to join the armed services where they will gain discipline, self esteem and learn a trade.

Take a tougher stance against recidivist criminals who reject rehabilitation opportunities. We mustn't let gangs run prisons.

Develop a New Zealand-wide strategy to beat the gangs, before it is too late. It is pointless continuing with the policing tactics of the 1960s and 70s, because the size and shape of the problem has changed dramatically.

Never negotiate with gangs. We should not seek their co-operation.

Create a National Crime Authority that brings together the police, Inland Revenue, Customs, Department of Correc-tions, Labour Department, Immigration Service, Ministry of Foreign Affairs and Trade, and even the Security Intelligence Service.

Develop new types of punishment for gang members who commit crime.

Ensure that gangs are not reinforced by taxpayer-subsidised work schemes. It is unacceptable that the government keeps no records of the numbers of gang members on work schemes. We should have the guts to get rid of schemes and projects that fail. No taxpayer money should be handed out unless people leave gangs.

Stop gangs from intimidating witnesses and the police.

Ensure that the justice system is legally accountable for the way it treats victims of crime.

Every Cabinet paper must have attached to it a Treasury report; so a similar report ought also to be received on how each decision affects families and children.

index